In fascinating, easy-to-read case histories based on revealing interviews, more than fifty people talk openly—and often heatedly— about the highly charged father/ child relationships in their lives.

- **How do children "turn out" when their fathers want them to follow in their own footsteps?

- **What effect does a seductive father have on his daughter's sexuality?

- **Why do the sons and daughters of demanding fathers frequently have difficulties in their careers and relationships?

- **When is one child's account of his father likely to differ from that of his brother or sister?

- **Does an eccentric father's outrageous behavior always affect his children?

Finally, you can understand the profound influence of your father's personality on your life as a child . . . and as an adult.

FATHERS:

DAUGHTERS, SONS, FATHERS
REVEAL THEIR DEEPEST FEELINGS

Robert Meister

BALLANTINE BOOKS • NEW YORK

Library of Congress Catalog Card Number: 80-28907

ISBN 0-345-30482-9

This edition published by arrangement with Richard Marek Publishers, Inc.

Manufactured in the United States of America

First Ballantine Books Edition: November 1983

To Christine

contents

introduction

Information about fathers is astonishingly scant in the literature of psychology and the social sciences; for every published article on father-child relationships there are fifteen dealing with mother-child bonds, and for each entry for father in the indexes of books addressed to developmental studies and family structure there are at least seven, and often as many as thirty, entries for mother. A number of books have been published on the continuing education of fathers, urging them to do a better job and telling them how to go about it—a genre known under the awkward label of "fathering"—but compared to the literature of advice and instruction for women and mothers, they are minute in quantity. Although social scientists have often studied men's work roles, religious and political beliefs, and leisure habits, notably in relation to sports, their role as father has had exceptionally low priority for inquiry. Furthermore, such information as there is about fathers has been usually obtained secondhand, from wives and children.

The chief reason for the disproportionate treatment of

mothers and fathers is the neglected fact that manliness is definitely not identified with fatherhood, whereas womanliness is very often equated with motherliness, even in the relatively enlightened climate of today's western industrial societies. Notions of motherhood are firmly fixed in these societies, but the criteria of fatherhood vary from place to place.

The disparity of the situation was further aggravated in recent years by the blossoming of feminist literature with its emphasis on the role of the mother and its neglect of or hostility toward the father. I felt that the time had come to find out what fathers have to say about their children and vice versa, to explore the interaction between fathers and children and the feelings that constitute it. This ruled out a book on ''fathering,'' or one about the father's role in family dynamics or social theory; the book had to be about the *subjective* experience of being a father and having one, about the infinite ways daughters and sons feel about their father now and felt about him at earlier stages of their lives, as well as about the corresponding feelings of fathers toward their children.

These realistic considerations ran parallel to my intense personal feelings of failure as a son and father. I came to realize that being a son or daughter includes a sense of responsibility, akin to that of the father's and no less weighty. Although the psychological literature makes no mention of such a responsibility, I am convinced that my failure to make an intensive effort to get to know my father injected a noxious substance into my subsequent relationships with my own children—a conviction reinforced later by numerous others. Furthermore, posthumous attempts to analyze and make sense of one's relationship with father do not make up for the failure of not having made such attempts while he was alive. A residue of regret carries over into one's own fatherhood, placing a veil between father and children, a veil that must be pierced from *both sides,* or else it survives into the next generation.

Once the objective and subjective needs to explore the raw material of father-child relations had made themselves clearly felt, I began to talk to others, first informally, later systematically. The book that emerged is based on 213 interviews; in 98 of these, fathers talked about their children, and the rest is roughly equally divided between sons and daughters talking about their fathers. In 40 cases, two or more siblings viewed their father in separate interviews, and in 52 instances father-son and father-daughter pairs spoke separately about each other.

Special effort was made to obtain ethnic, geographical, and socioeconomic balance, and the published accounts reflect the demographic realities of America in 1981.

The average duration of an interview was two hours. Eighty-five percent were conducted by asking questions and either tape recording or writing down the answers; fifteen percent chose to tape record what they had to say in private. These solitary reflections tended to be quite long; one father recorded five hours of material, and two- to three-hour accounts were common. Everyone was acquainted with the purpose of the interview before agreeing to do it; nevertheless, identifiable circumstances were carefully altered.

It was the rule rather than the exception for people to recall long-forgotten episodes from the past during the course of the interview and long-repressed emotions welled up with striking regularity. It was, therefore, not surprising that a random follow-up revealed that a highly significant percentage of interviewees entered some sort of therapeutic regimen within a few months of the interview. Virtually all volunteered the information that they had been impelled to reexamine their relationships with their father.

Soon after the interviewing process began, it became obvious that the material would have to be filtered in an arbitrary way. It made no sense to try to force subjective experiences into channels that had objective criteria, because it would have turned the book into one with figures and tables. Subjective experiences reveal themselves best when they are presented on their own terms, which meant setting up categories like "distant" and "macho" that are themselves subjective. They are, in other words, my categories, and there is no question in my mind that another writer would have chosen different ones.

The interviews showed that the range of feelings between fathers and children is infinite, and any attempt to synthesize the material would be doomed. It is only when one compares the recurring themes of father-child bonds in the literature of fiction, especially English and Russian, with the principal themes that emerged in the interviews that certain general observations can be made. In novels, father-child conflicts are commonly caused by the distance between maturity and adolescence, authority and revolt, convention and new mores, and the battlegrounds are sexual, vocational, religious, and financial. As Sir Douglas Hubble has observed, hundreds of autobiographies have been written by suffering sons—but only a few by daughters—after they have escaped paternal control. The diaries of James Boswell, for example, are filled with accounts of the contests between himself and his father, Lord Auchinleck, which were conducted on all four fronts.

The recurring themes that emerged from the interviews are more immediate and explicit, perhaps because they are rooted in real life, whereas literature deals with the vapors that rise from it. Availability, communication, and expectations are the principal themes, along with masculinity/ femininity, self-confidence/achievement, morals/discipline, social/sexual relationships, and competence/work/career. The categories I finally decided upon seemed to contain these essential themes more readily and dramatically than did others that were considered and dismissed.

The first category, distant and silent fathers, is probably the saddest, because it focuses on the motifs of availability, communication, and mutual expectations in a negative atmosphere. Feelings remain unexpressed for these people, they rankle and ulcerate; signals are transmitted faultily and misperceived, leading to festering bitterness; acts or the absence of acts are misconstrued, creating residues of resentment.

Seductive fathers, the second category, affect the social and sexual relationships of daughters most of all, again in a negative sense. I have not been able to find a daughter of a seductive father who attained sexual stability without having gone through demoralizing, humiliating experiences, and the number of those who do attain stability is rather small.

Tyrannical, demanding fathers come in the widest variety of all. Some are subtle, others brutal, with many shadings between the two extremes, and they affect all areas of the developing personality of their children. They are all too available and communicate explicitly, but their influence on the child's self-confidence, morals, sexuality, and career can be devastating. Those children who do attain success pay a heavy price in emotional damage.

Children who idealize their fathers are most likely to achieve stable, unharmed lives, even if the fathers are unworthy of idealization by objective standards. It seems to matter little whether the father is saintly or roguish, for the child clings only to the traits that are desirable and ignores the rest.

Macho-competitive fathers differ from tyrannical-demanding ones in that they are not repressive, although they can be oppressive indeed. They are seldom successful in bringing up their children in their own image, although when they have three children or more, one is likely to be macho-competitive—usually a son.

It is difficult to generalize about bizarre-eccentric fathers, because by definition they seldom have anything in common. For mundane reasons, only one such father could be included, but, if the material contained in the unpublished interviews is an indication, their children are not necessarily marked by the fathers' eccentricities.

What struck me most in the course of completing this book is the discrepancy of accounts offered by siblings and also by fathers and children. The picture painted by a brother and sister of their common father can be stunningly different to the point that one is not certain that they are talking about the same person, and events described by father and child are often discordant, even totally contradictory. It is not always possible to identify the truth, and perhaps it does not matter. Denial, distortion, and self-delusion all serve the purpose of defending the self from anguish; on that point, life and literature do converge.

distant, silent

Anna is thirty-two. She lives in a large city, absorbed in smoking dope, in television, in herself. She is alone and works only long enough in any job to qualify for unemployment. She is strikingly attractive but hardly ever goes out with men. She has been divorced for seven years; her occasional liaisons are restricted to men who are unavailable owing to more binding attachments or unsteady temperament.

Anna sleeps twelve to fourteen hours a day, reads *People* and the *National Enquirer*, lacks motivation, ambition, and joy, yet in company she is charming, interesting, and sharply humorous. Her education was routine and she has retained little learning. She is by no means well read and her knowledge of the world is sketchy. She could not find Ecuador on the map, not even Austria. She has never been outside the United States and has no knowledge of languages.

Nevertheless, her opinions on most matters are firmly held and resistant to outside influence. To outward appearances, she is self-assured, confident, even strident, and there is no doubt that she is keenly observant of physical details and more than ordinarily perceptive to nuances of the psychology and behavior of others. She could have had promising careers half a dozen times; she is regarded by former employers and others as sharp, smart, and efficient. It is her self-defined melancholia that has been keeping her at the bare level of self-sustenance.

Anna's marriage lasted six years by the calendar but substantially shorter by more reliable indicators. She used to claim that her bond to her husband was so complex, so deep, so ''special'' that it could not be explained or even intimated to outsiders. She was convinced the marriage would last forever, although those who had known the couple thought otherwise. What they had seen appeared to be game playing, self-delusion; the marriage lacked a perceptible core. It was not a bond but a temporary alliance of two very young and inexperienced people against the shifting winds.

But these observations are held by others and their validity is uncertain. To Anna, now, the marriage is a hazy memory, and on the rare occasions when her former husband's name comes up, it is usually accompanied by sardonic and sarcastic remarks. It is not a subject she is wont to discuss, but it is clear that the experience has left her with a degree of malaise.

The history of Anna's other significant relationships with men is largely in the same vein. Her first great love in high school was elusive and ultimately unattainable, and his successors no less so. If they had another quality in common, it was their itinerancy: Actors gave way to chefs, to exchange students, to married men—all made exciting by unavailability and ephemerality.

Sexually, Anna claims to be rather passionate and to have no patience for men who are not—a claim advanced by the fact that her former husband is known to be a womanizer and a sensualist. At the same time, frequent remarks confirm the suspicion that sexual activity is usually if not invariably carried out in a cloud of marijuana or on the wings of cocaine. Of sexual fantasies she says nothing.

Anna has not spoken to her father in three years, nor

heard from him. She does not expect an imminent change in the situation, and when she is cajoled into talking about him, her tone is bitter and highly emotional. She believes that her father, Roger, once a dashing, romantic free spirit, has turned into a boring bourgeois hedonist whose inherent hedonism has been transformed from its previous form of search for lust, for freedom from conventional responsibilities, for an unencumbered life, to one of search for good restaurants, possessions, and unusual vacation places.

Anna's current feelings began to develop some seven years ago when Roger married his present wife, after twenty years as a divorced man involved with an endless succession of women of infinite variety. She had met most of them and says she liked all but one whose age was much too close to her own. She was even proud of her father's appeal for women, encouraged his pursuits, and bragged about him to her friends. During the ten-year period following her graduation from high school, Anna and Roger were extraordinarily close, often talking on the telephone for hours, late into the night. She would confide in him completely, revealing matters she would never think of sharing with her mother, whom, she claims, she has always hated and despised. She smoked grass uninhibitedly in his company, and he often joined her. They discussed everything freely, except for matters relating to sex. Once, high on grass, she did ask him how her mother was in bed and he told her she was hot but inhibited, which, Anna says, made her unaccountably happy.

This idyllic period fell under a dark cloud when Roger remarried. His wife was an earthy, no-nonsense, successful and independent woman whose liking for Anna was unreserved and clearly demonstrated. At first, the atmosphere of sympathy and affection was mutual, and Anna remembers feeling distinctly that it was time her father settled down, as he was in his late fifties, and that he could not have chosen a better partner. She did not notice at the time that the dissolution of her own marriage took place concurrently with the establishment of her father's, and when questioned on this point seven years later, she denied any connection between the two events. Indignantly, she turned away the unspoken implications of the subject by stating that she has never ever felt any physical attraction to Roger, even though she recognized and even prided herself in his attractiveness to other women. (During our many conversations, she consistently referred to her father by his given name only.)

After the glow of Roger's marriage wore off for Anna, she began to develop resentments directed at him. The long telephone talks became scarcer and scarcer, and when Roger took her out for dinner—a frequent event—he was not alone with Anna any longer; his wife was always with them. She also noted that his lifelong devil-may-care attitude about money was visibly changing; under the influence of his realistic wife, he was paying more attention to making money and subsequently had more of it. Although Anna considered this development an undesirable change in his character, a corruption of a romantic, she admits that she unaccountably yearned to share in it. She relieved this feeling by initiating a habit of asking for and receiving what she invariably called ''loans,'' and intentionally failing to repay them.

Roger and his wife, Norma, were fond of giving elegant dinner parties to which Anna was always invited—another corrupting development. She strongly felt that she was being regarded merely as ''Roger's daughter,'' and was indeed often introduced as such. She abruptly left one party after being told that she had her father's sense of humor. Her father's friends, all newly acquired, struck Anna as being excessively materialistic, and as time went on she became more and more abrasive toward them. She is well aware now that her hostility was a safety valve that drained off her feelings before they could be directed at their true object— the transformed Roger, the formerly beloved father now turning into a bourgeois clown.

Slowly but inexorably the situation became too strained to be sustained, and one night, while Roger was criticizing her behavior on the telephone, she abruptly hung up on him. There has been no direct or indirect communication between them since then.

Anna admits that she often thinks about her father as he

used to be. She clearly remembers their affectionate rough-housing when she was quite little, and how she liked to comb and brush his hair, playing hairdresser. She also remembers the sudden shock of her parents' divorce when she was six and the rapturous excitement of waiting for him on his scheduled visiting days. When her mother sent her to a remote boarding school that was virtually inaccessible during winters, making visits preciously rare, she was angry and frustrated. She interpreted her mother's action as one of sheer vindictiveness directed against Roger, as if she had been hiding Anna from him. All through her school years, and for many years after, Anna saw herself as being in an alliance with Roger, the two of them against her mother, united and unbreachable.

This is not how Anna feels today. Today she feels betrayed and abandoned by her father. The divorce is now perceived as an abandonment, and his failure to snatch her away from the hated boarding school as a betrayal. She sees him today as an ungiving, remote, disapproving person—an enemy. When asked to explain the transformation of her feelings from uncritical love to affection and intimacy to rejection, she attributed it first and foremost to the intolerable changes in her father's life, character, and personality. At the same time, she regards herself as more mature and perceptive now than she has ever been before and believes that her present views, both subjective and objective, are accurate. She sees little chance of reconciliation.

When Anna was asked to consider the possibility that her present state of physical and psychological lethargy, whether stemming from or resulting in habitual abuse of marijuana and cocaine, may be distorting her feelings toward her father, she was quick to deny it. In fact, for the first time in our conversations, she introduced the theme that her way of life today is the direct result of her father's rejection of her. Even though it was she who caused the breach between them, it is evident that just as she was hoping to be rescued by him from her exile in school—a vain and frustrated hope—so does she now hope to be saved by him from her exile from life, setting herself up for what she perceives to be betrayal and abandonment once again.

Roger is in his early sixties now and lives in the same city as his daughter, Anna. He is a free-lance designer, doing as well as he needs to do. He has been happily married for seven years and has given up womanizing for flirting. He is a classically educated European intellectual who came to America after World War II; he has many interests, travels widely, and speaks several languages—accomplishments he failed to pass on to Anna or were scorned by her. A streak of melancholia, so eagerly embraced by his daughter, reveals itself only when triggered by certain subjects, such as Anna or his own long-dead father.

He lacks Anna's strident self-assurance; he is thoughtful, intense, often witty. He tends to be excessively self-effacing to the point of sometimes irritating those around him. His physical resemblance to Anna is as startling as are the disparities between them.

His ambivalence on many subjects is all too evident and he seems to relish it as an antidote to a closed mind. At times, his conversation turns into lecturing, which is both annoying and edifying. He has led an eventful life inordinately touched by tragedy and irony, and feels very sad about the fact, as he sees it, that his daughter has never expressed any interest in it. He claims to have many distant acquaintances, virtual strangers, who know more details of his life than does his own daughter. This seems to be a matter of profound sorrow to him. When it is suggested to him that his aloof demeanor might discourage personal inquiries, he replies that if people want to know each other, they must persistently, patiently, and discreetly probe for answers, and that this is especially imperative for children in relation to their parents. He himself feels an acute sense of failure for not having gotten to know his father, for not even having made the effort.

He has two recurrent dreams about his father, who has been dead now for forty years. In one, his father would come to his bed while he was sleeping, lean over him, and watch him silently with sad, serious eyes. In the other, he dreams about walking in a strange city, then suddenly stopping because his father would be approaching from the opposite direction. As in a movie, his face would grow larger with every step, and he would come very close, open his now immense lips, and say something not heard by the dreamer which explains life with a single word.

Roger grew up in central Europe at a time when nineteenth-century customs and mores were still deeply embedded in family life. In the upper and upper-middle classes, to which his family belonged, the life of parents was almost entirely separated from that of children. Children were brought up and nurtured by nannies, servants, and later tutors, the mother would visit them once a day in midafternoon—called the "children's hour"—while the father might not be seen for days or even weeks at a time. His role was mainly a punitive one, but even that was reserved for major retributions only. For most children, he was feared the way "primitive" people fear natural disasters.

Roger's father was a substantial landowner whose family tree was rooted in the fourteenth century, and he was married to the only daughter of a Jewish family of considerable wealth. He was almost constantly away supervising his estates, while Roger's mother was occupied with the demands of social life. The first wave of emotion the boy ever felt came over him upon the departure of a beloved nanny, the first feeling of love evoked not by the embrace of his mother but by the kiss bestowed on him by his piano teacher when he was six, and she probably thirty-five. As psychological wisdom tells us, love and affection must be learned, and if Roger learned, it was from strangers.

His memories of his father are exceedingly scant. The first occurred when he must have been at least five, and it still lies deep, behind all memories, he says nearly sixty years later. He was sitting on the floor of his room, playing with a toy drum. His father came in, something that had never happened before, and sat down on the floor beside him. The boy's first thought was that his father must have gone mad; grownups did not sit on the floor. Then, suddenly, his father began to sing: *"Joli tambour . . . donnez moi vôtre coeur . . ."* The song came from behind his huge teeth, and his face was strangely contorted as his lips opened and closed.

The boy understood instinctively that his father wanted to make good for everything—for the silence, the absence, the solitude, the distance. He wanted to solve everything with one gesture, by sitting down on the floor and singing a folk song. There was a statue in the main square of the town, a giant bronze soldier pointing his spear at the heart of the tyrant; the boy felt that the statue had jumped down from its pedestal and was crawling on its hands and knees in full armor.

"Vôtre coeur . . ." he repeated with trembling lips to console his father, for whom he now felt a great compassion. He began to cry. His father rose slowly, walked around the room as if he had been looking for something all along, then noticed the child watching him through his tears, shrugged his shoulders slightly, and left the room. They did not look into each other's eyes for a long time after this, like two accomplices in a common, humiliating lie.

On the rare occasions when the father was home, once or twice a month, he would lock himself in his study and practice the violin. He never learned to play it; perhaps bashfulness or stubbornness had kept him from taking lessons. He fought the instrument for an hour or more, drawing painful sounds from it. He played badly and, Roger felt, maliciously. The recurring, determined struggle with the violin seemed to the boy as if his father had abandoned himself to an ugly and shameful passion with the candid knowledge of his household. Whenever he could, Roger too would lock himself in his room at such times, sit in the dark, and press his hands against his ears, waiting for the sounds to end.

The only time in his life when Roger spent as much as a

full week with his father occurred in 1936, when they attended the Olympic Games in Berlin together. To Roger's astonishment—he was now nineteen—his father appeared for their first dinner on the arms of two stunning young women. Although it was customary at the time for fathers, even mothers, of the middle and upper classes to have lovers, the subject had never been mentioned in Roger's presence and his knowledge of the matter derived solely from observation and talks with friends. He felt awkward during dinner and excused himself early, having noticed that his father never looked at him and excluded him from the table talk almost entirely.

Late that night, one of the women admitted herself to Roger's room. She came, she said, because his father wanted her to find out if he was still a virgin; if he was, she was to initiate him, if he was not, then she was to be a gift from father to son. Shocked by the sudden transformation of his distant father into a carnal comrade, Roger pretended to be a virgin still, although he had been sexually active since thirteen. He submitted to her sublime expertise and instructions, which she seemed to enjoy imparting as much as he did receiving. For the rest of their stay, the unforgettable Karin continued to guide him to more and more advanced and complex delights each night, while remaining invisible during the days. His father largely avoided him throughout the Games, letting him find his own way, and gave no hint of knowing anything. On the day of their scheduled departure, Roger found a note at the desk instructing him to proceed home; his father had further business in Berlin and would follow in a week or so.

There was virtually no personal communication between father and son from that time on. In 1939, a few weeks before the outbreak of World War II, Roger's parents were divorced and his father married the daughter of a leading local Nazi soon after. This act left Roger's Jewish mother unprotected by his father's influential connections against the rapidly multiplying complications of being Jewish in a Nazi Europe. Roger—himself officially Jewish by the tenets of the Nürnberg laws—sided completely with his mother and they took an apartment together. All contact between father and son ceased. In 1942, he was summoned to his father's deathbed by a manservant but, despite his mother's urgings, he refused to go, nor did he attend the funeral. Within months, he was on his way to the first of many concentration camps.

When he returned home at war's end, he found that his mother had been killed in an air raid, her family gassed in Auschwitz, and his father's estate, now rightfully his, confiscated by the new regime. After some tribulations, he arrived in America at age thirty, untutored in love, drained of emotions, mentally arid—a manchild in a strange land.

Having already embarked on a career in design while still in Europe, Roger's only goal at the time was to immerse himself in work; as he now sees it, he did not want to think or feel, only to do. But this was not to be. He met an American woman, some years older than he was, who appeared to be kind, understanding, tender. She was one of many children of an industrial working-class family who has managed to break away from her soot-stifled midwestern native town and make a modest, decent career on her own as an administrative assistant.

Roger was the first European she had met, but he was no more exotic to her than she was to him. The simple act of eating dinners in her kitchen—a locale he had never even set foot in—became a sort of anthropological adventure for him, and washing or drying dishes was positively exhilarating. For Helen's part, she found his Old World manners, his frequent references and allusions to matters unknown to her, his occasional sadnesses, captivating. He introduced an unexpected dimension to her life that was both exciting and disturbing, while she became his navigator in waters he might not have been able to manage on his own.

Soon after they met, she asked him to marry her. He was totally unprepared for the offer, and even more so for the state it entailed: He had never seen a working model of a marriage. He never witnessed the details of his parents' marriage; he had little or no idea of how a marriage *worked*. What was expected of one? And of the other? What exactly did one contribute to make a marriage workable, even possibly happy?

He had never discussed these questions with married friends and had given them no previous thought. He vaguely supposed that people were afraid of being alone, or wanted children, but never related these thoughts to his own life. When he sought Helen's answer to these questions, she was soothing and spoke in generalities; she used words like "love," "happiness," and "family"—imprecise words for him, words known only from literature. Yet, he trusted literature. "Love" might lead to uncontrollable situations and tragedies, as it did for Werther and Anna Karenina and Romeo, but at least it contained passion for which he yearned, and "happiness" and "family" reminded him of Tolstoy and contained the promise of salvation.

Roger now says that these intellectual considerations did in fact play an important part in persuading him to marry Helen; they impelled him to discover, to attempt to discover, within himself emotions and experiences that were real and true in others. But he also admits that he was incapable of making decisions at that period of his life; he had become accustomed during the war to being overtaken by events beyond his control. Life for him was a state of suspension where one awaited the next episode; it was desirable always to be prepared, but it was impossible to act.

And so the marriage took place, and ten months later Anna was born. She was neither planned nor unwanted and, at first, Roger was unmoved but interested. His home was also his workplace, and he spent a great deal of time observing the infant. Soon he was actively participating in her care, particularly in the ritual of diaper change, which struck him as being organic and aesthetic at the same time. The tiny body, its simple needs and demands, filled him with wonder; he was beginning to develop a capacity for warmth and caring. He was able to give his child what he never received from his parents: manifestations of physical affection and, at long last, love. He learned to love backwards, as it were; while most of us learn to love by first receiving it and then giving, Roger learned by giving and then slowly attaining the capacity of receiving.

His marriage was not a good one; Helen suffered from pathological, as yet unjustified, jealousy, and she made scenes at every opportunity. She was also, by Roger's account, a manic depressive, dividing his life into predictable cycles of unhappiness where little Anna was the sole fixed point of gratification.

Roger remembers the first five years of Anna's life as probably the most important period in his life. He learned not only to feel but also to convey what he felt. The complex system of self-repression—a combination of social conventions and intellectual discipline—which characterized his behavior until then, dissolved during those years. He cried for the first time in his life the night he realized that his marriage had been intolerable and would have to be severed, with the consequence of his not being able to spend as much time with Anna as he had been spending for five years.

When he is asked now whether it might have been better for him to hold on to the marriage for the sake of maintaining his bond with Anna, his child, he is certain that it would not have worked. He believes that people who remain in bad marriages for the children's sake ultimately pay an even greater price; the role of the self-sacrificing parent is not only self-destructive but leads eventually to condemnation by the children or child.

And so he divorced Helen when Anna was between five and six, and the next ten years introduced some of the corrosive elements that were to lead to their present alienation. His visitation rights were limited beyond legal definitions by Helen's variable moods; during the first two years of divorce she would occasionally demand sex before letting him see Anna, and at other times extort money, thus insidiously affecting the tone and quality of the time father and daughter did spend together. He realized that Anna sensed his anger and would probably take it as if it had been directed at her, but he could do nothing about it. The demands of fatherhood and the exactions of selfhood are often at odds, he realized, and the damage will lie more heavily on the child.

Anna's recollections of this period are not inconsistent with Roger's. She blamed her mother for the divorce, and her father's visits were all the more precious, even when he seemed to be preoccupied. She still feels a sharp pang at the memory of the Sunday when, ordered to wait in her room, she listened to her mother berating Roger as she usually did, but this time her outburst was followed by a brief silence and then by a strange, seemingly painful moaning. Alarmed, she ran into the living room to find her mother lying on top of her father on the floor, making strange motions. She knew immediately that she was hurting him and screamed at her mother, "Stop it, stop hurting Daddy!"—and ran from the room in tears.

During the first two years of the divorce, Anna recalls, she first began to experience the pressure of expectations from her father. Until she was about seven, her father simply loved her, she feels, and expected nothing but love from her. While she was in second grade, she found that the nature of their Sundays together began to change. Physical fun in zoos and parks gave way to increasingly serious probing by Roger about school. He wanted to know in great detail what she was learning, how she was being taught, what she was not learning, and why. She remembers one painful afternoon spent on a park bench, her father insistently and morosely drilling her in the secrets of Roman numerals. She did not understand. He was also increasingly critical of her teachers, and spent more and more of their time on instructing her in subjects that were inadequately dealt with or untouched in school, he believed. She grew resentful and resisted his teaching. She felt that her father was disappointed in her lack of interest in acquiring knowledge; she felt that his love was turning into expectations of achievement.

Roger does not deny Anna's account but sees it in a different light. After his separation from his daughter, deprived of his love object, he began to "dry out" emotionally, to revert to his previous self-repression and intellectual discipline. He tacked up a quote from Dr. Johnson above his work table: "Accurate thought, serious study, continuous self-command," and admits that he began to expect others and, above all, his daughter, to live up to his demanding, emotionally sterile standards. Unrealistically and cold-bloodedly, he now knows, he expected Anna to joyously embrace learning which was force-fed into him during the painful years of his classical education. He acquired his knowledge mainly through fear, and he was now, perhaps, unconsciously getting his revenge by trying to force his daughter into the same pattern. He expected her to be intellectually curious, eager to learn, scholarly, and, ultimately, brilliant. Her resistance angered him and began to put a distance between them.

Clearly, the perceptions of Roger and Anna were accurate to the extent that he realized his anger and disappointment, as did she; however, the silence between them prevented her from learning what impelled him to behave as he did, as it prevented him from finding the reasons for her resistance. The wedge was now in place, to be driven deeper and deeper as time passed.

The distance between them and the silence grew during her forced exile in the remote boarding school of her teens. She bitterly resented his failure to rescue her, and still does, and he was increasingly involved in his career and his love affairs. He was hoping that after her graduation their lives would converge again, that she would be eager to know him as he believed he knew himself, that her resistance to his guidance would end.

Anna says she continued to love her father during those years and still felt that he loved her, but her belief that he was disappointed in her grew stronger and stronger. During vacations she spent time with him at his ever changing domiciles with his ever changing mistresses, and often they had good times together. Still, there was silence; needs, desires, feelings were not discussed, and she continued to feel the pressures of his expectations, which now expanded to choices of college and careers. The presence of his women, all of whom seemed to have interesting and rewarding occupations, aggravated her feelings, even though she grew to like one of these women to the point where she saw her and Roger as an ideal couple.

Anna began dating heavily after graduation from high school, and the men tended to be transient foreigners or otherwise elusive. Her resistance to going to college or choosing a career strengthened, and she started using drugs at this time. She took insignificant temporary jobs and experimented heavily with sex. She recalls, almost proudly, one particular job where her lunch hours were spent in having stand-up sex in the supply room. She was living with her mother in a suburb, having bitter, violent fights, and her contacts with Roger became scarce.

One day, she suddenly decided to enter a tiny unaccredited college in southern California, in spite of the fact that her father's connections at that time were so good that she would have been admitted to the best colleges in the land. There was occasional telephone contact and visits during vacations, but feelings were now completely repressed by both. From time to time, she tried to shock Roger by intimations of heavy acid tripping and grass smoking, even hints at lesbian inclinations. Roger failed to respond with alarm, not for lack of concern, as she perceived it, but because he tried to avoid reacting the way fathers were supposed to react to unwelcome news. He preferred to react sympathetically, as a friend rather than as a parent. Thus, their distance and silence betrayed them once again. Her signals were misinterpreted by him, his reactions misread by her.

She then married the young man she had been tripping with—a step that agitated Roger. He could not understand the reasons for a marriage as cohabitation was widely practiced if not accepted by the late 1960s; besides, Anna had consistently proclaimed her decision not to have children. But he said nothing, and the couple moved into the suburban apartment given them by her mother. For the duration of the marriage, there were frequent, long late-night telephone conversations, but Roger always had the suspicion that Anna was invariably high during these talks. Again, he said nothing, although he felt sure that the drug taking masked a silent despair, a scream he did not want to hear.

The end of Anna's marriage and the beginning of Roger's marked the beginning of their present alienation, which does

21

not seem to abate. The father is silently angry at his daughter's failure to make any effort to know him, and disappointed by her lethargy, her lack of interest in anything that interests him. The daughter is silently furious at having been abandoned, although she will not admit it; she masks her fury with contempt for what she sees as her father's transformation from a free spirit into a bourgeois hedonist.

This relationship, prototypically distant and silent, is aggravated chiefly by cultural disparities that neither father nor daughter attempted to bridge, by misdirected and misperceived expectations that remained always unspoken and, most seriously, by the apparent unwillingness of either to take even a single step toward the other.

Distance and silence are innate elements of Roger's nature, adopted from his father, and probably culturally determined. In Victorian upper-class life, children were often objects, to be molded according to standards devised for them by their parents, principally their fathers. This is the only model Roger was familiar with, and it suited him temperamentally—a realization that came to him too late. Had it come earlier, he would have been able to bridge the cultural gap between himself and his daughter, and Anna would not have misperceived his expectations as unreasonable demands, when in fact they were Roger's expression of love.

Love is clearly not an inborn emotion like fear. It must be learned in infancy and childhood, or else it may never be learned at all—a thesis illustrated in Roger's life. By the time he learned, in taking care of his infant daughter, it might have been already too late. For love to be effective, it has to be psychologically useful—otherwise, it does not work. It is not enough to feel it, or even to verbalize it, if its form is not useful to the object of love. Certainly, Roger's love was strikingly not useful to Anna.

The effect of silent, distant fathers on their children is

probably more insidious than either physical brutality or psychological tyranny. Silence and distance are breeding grounds of festering misunderstandings that can only become more and more noxious in time.

George is twenty-eight, a successful importer, contentedly settled in a five-year-old relationship, of optimistic outlook and pleasant disposition, extremely fond of his father, on good terms with his mother; on the whole, one of the happiest and stablest persons one is likely to meet. Yet, he considers his father as having always been distant and silent; also, George is homosexual.

George's brother, Tom, is five years older, a satisfied husband, doting father of two, somewhat cynical in his attitude toward the affairs of the world, an upwardly mobile middle-level corporate executive, bitter and resentful about his father, very close to his mother, stable in his personal and business lives, but emotionally volatile inward. He also considers his father as distant and will not forgive him for it; he blames him for George's homosexuality, which he finds "sick."

James, their father, is in his late fifties and has run a "mom and pop" store with his wife for some thirty-five years. He is a quiet man, polite and minimally friendly, difficult to talk to; he opens up only after a few glasses of red wine, at which point he becomes voluble. His wife is very friendly, open, and obviously bossy. He professes not to mind George's homosexuality; in fact, he admits that George was always his favorite.

Tom claims not to remember anything before his brother was born, but he clearly recalls placing a blanket over the baby's crib, for which act he received a solid spanking from his mother; his father only smiled. Tom says he tried consistently to elicit his father's attention throughout his school years, sometimes with accomplishments, sometimes with misdeeds. The results were meager, although they invariably evoked response from his mother; while this was pleasing, it was somewhat inadequate. Tom could not believe that a smile, a frown, a pat on the head, a few words of praise or disapproval, were proper reactions to his efforts. They were not "fatherly" somehow. His friends' fathers were quite different; some were tyrannical, others friendly, some were quick to punish misbehavior, others were reasonable. In their own ways, they seemed to guide their sons' lives; in turn, they were admired, feared, respected, imitated, complained and bragged about. Their existence had a firm bearing on the sons' lives; they could not be disregarded or circumvented. Tom felt that his father was ephemeral; it was easy to pretend that he did not exist at all.

Tom cannot remember a single instance of playing with his father, either in the house or outside; the sentence he recalls hearing most often was, "Go outside and play." His brother was much too young to be of use as a playmate, and, later, too young to be a friend, a confidant. He was merely in the way, taking up a lot of mother's time, distracting father even more. Nor does Tom remember having a substantial conversation with his father, although his mother was always available for a talk. Yet, it was not the same; discussions with mother seemed like messages, communiqués, to be relayed to father and then returned with his seal of approval or disapproval. But nothing was ever returned, there was only silence.

Tom was often told by his mother that he should become an accountant, and he often asked his father what he thought of it. "That would be nice," came the answer, encouraging but uncompelling. It did not seem to Tom that becoming an accountant would admit him into his father's confidence or make him an object of greater interest than he was. Yet, he believed that there had to be something to accomplish this.

As a teenager, Tom became unruly and developed into a "problem." He dabbled in petty crimes like hubcap lifting, joyrides in temporarily stolen cars, and shoplifting in dime stores. He was arrested a few times, but nothing serious ever resulted. He was always remanded in the care of his parents, which led to interminable lectures from his mother in the silent, disapproving presence of his father, looking doleful and disappointed. On the two worst occasions, his mother whipped him with a belt borrowed from his father, who stood by holding up his pants with his hands, shaking his head.

For a couple of years during his early teens, he would get out of bed almost every night and listen at his parents' bedroom door. About once a week, he would hear strange sounds coming from his mother, as if she were in pain but not alarmingly so and never for long; he heard no sounds from his father ever. He soon expanded his activities by prowling about the neighborhood and looking in windows; eventually, he had seen enough to be able to interpret the sounds his mother made. Supplemented by information from his friends, his observations formed the core of his sex education.

He began to develop elaborate sexual fantasies based on his secretly acquired knowledge. The male principal was always his father, and he had him perform superhuman sexual feats with beautiful women he had seen in magazines or in the streets, some of them customers in his father's store. The fantasies always began with his father's showing his enormous penis to the various women who would then swoon into helpless submissiveness, allowing him to take them with ferocious ardor that lasted until Tom was able to attain masturbatory orgasm. Sometimes his mother figured in these fantasies, but always in the same role: She would beg her husband for his sexual favors on her knees, which he would refuse most of the time, leaving her sobbing on the floor. Rarely, the request would be granted, but in one way only: He would unzip his pants and allow her to gratify herself orally while he stood there indifferently and patronizingly.

Tom understands clearly that his accomplishments, misdeeds, and fantasies were all directed at calling his father's attention to himself; unsuccessful though they were, he could not and did not want to stop. Even today, himself a father, he never fails to convey news of his successes; he has learned to report events to his father first and, having taken in his minimal responses, tell them to his mother separately and indulge in her profuse enthusiasm.

When Tom was eighteen, he discovered to his horror that his brother George was "queer." He found the boy lying naked on his bed with a naked friend, masturbating each other. He became so enraged at the sight that he took off his belt and whipped both boys raw. He then rushed downstairs to the store, took his father into the storeroom and told him what had happened. He was sure that this time he would get his attention, even arouse him, even compel him to act. When he finished his report, his heart was pounding with excitement, waiting for the reactions he had expected. For what seemed like a long time, his father stood silently, and Tom can still recapture the shock he felt when his father finally spoke. "You whipped him with your belt?" he said. "You had no right to do that." When Tom demanded to know whether he was going to do anything about it, he said he would "speak to the boy."

Tom does not know to this day what his father said to George, although he does know that they spent a considerable time locked in the storeroom. George did not seem to be shaken afterward, nor did his father. "Keep your mother out of this," was all that was said.

Tom began to abuse his brother at every opportunity from that time on, both verbally and physically. The very idea of homosexuality was utterly incomprehensible to him and it started to interfere with his sexual fantasies; occasionally, images of his father and brother lying naked on a bed flashed through his mind, making him sick to his stomach. His sex life also became active, and he did not always enjoy it; he often needed to fantasize in order to get excited.

Tom says that for a period of about five years he was confused, even disturbed, by the demands of his sexuality; he could not sort things out. His desire for women was strong and they were attracted to him, but deep inside he was disturbed by the secret shame of George's homosexuality and by his father's apparent acceptance of it. He was also vexed by his brother's obvious equanimity; he did not look or act like a homosexual, and at the same time he seemed content to be one. As for his mother, if she knew about it at all, she certainly was not showing any signs of it.

During these years, he thought a lot about his family, and families in general. What held families together? Why did his mother, a strong, merry person, ever marry his ineffectual, inconsequential father? Why did she *need* him? How could his own brother, growing up under the same roof, with the same parents, become a homosexual? He was intensely occupied with these questions and tried to get some answers from books and friends. Books had no answers for Tom; they spun theories, made general observations, compared groups of people with other groups of people, but said nothing that he could apply to his own situation. Friends were more useful, and it was obvious that they had unanswered questions of their own. While he concealed his brother's homosexuality from them, they clearly had secrets in their families as well. After a bout of Saturday night drinking, his closest friend told Tom that he hated his father with a passion because he habitually beat his wife and children. Another friend hinted darkly that his mother received a lover during the day while her husband was at work. When Tom complained of his father's indifference and ineptitude, his friends told him to be glad; their own fathers were too strict, or too interfering, too controlling. They claimed they would have liked a father who left them alone, which made Tom feel somewhat better. Sill, there remained something inexplicable.

Meanwhile, Tom had followed his mother's urgings and studied for accountancy with a few occasional lapses and hesitations. He moved out of home as soon as he made enough money to maintain himself and gave up all contacts with his brother who was by now a scholarship student at a fine college, several hundred miles away. He visited his parents once a week, usually for dinner; he let his mother fuss over him and flood him with questions. He made a point of looking at his father while answering his mother's questions, as if to compel him not only to listen but also to acknowledge him. He was seldom successful; if his father asked him any questions at all, they related to his dating. Contrary to what he had heard from his friends, it was his father who seemed interested in seeing him get married—a subject shunned by his mother completely. He was not exactly pressuring him, but about once a month he would inquire when Tom planned to get married. When in turn Tom asked him why he was so interested in seeing him married, he invariably remarked that a man ought to be married, have children, and live to see his grandchildren. When asked why this should be so, he said it was "in the nature of things."

In his late twenties, Tom did marry a young woman from a nearby town; she is very competent and quite ambitious for him. It was she who persuaded him to join a large company, and Tom has been moving up the corporate ladder steadily. They now have two children and Tom's life is quite steady, except for his remaining hostility for his father and rejection of his brother. When asked what kind of father he is to his own children, he says he is the exact opposite of his father. He spends most of his free time with them, takes constant interest in everything they do, and hovers about them a great deal. He has read a number of books on "fathering," and learned what is expected of him; he is bringing his children up by the book, as it were, and it was not possible to elicit any information from him about how he feels toward them. It appears certain that he will always try to do what is best for the children; unlike Roger, he at least has a model for loving in his mother, and while he may be too anxious right now to be his father's opposite, to do only the right things, to be a textbook father, it is more than probable that in the long run his children will feel loved by him.

George's account of his father is dramatically different from that of his brother. He does agree with Tom's assessment that their father was distant and silent, but views it in an entirely different light. He does not feel, as his brother does, that their father's attitude should be equated with indifference toward his children or with lack of love; even more importantly, he does not feel that it was a barrier that needed to be overcome by the children or a weapon aimed at them that had to be taken away from him.

George is convinced, and quotes Joyce to the effect, that his father's "silence and exile" was merely his mode of coping with the world, that he was probably deeply wounded by life early on but was incapable of healing himself, because, as George says, "he knew neither the tune nor the words." This romantic view probably saved George the agonies suffered by Tom, and for those who prefer literature to psychology it makes very good sense. When asked why he thinks that his father was probably deeply wounded by life, he replies that there is no other possibility, that people who are distant and silent have had no choice; they cannot trust the world enough to invest their feelings into it. When asked if he ever attempted to find out about his father's childhood and early life by asking him directly, he says no. He feels certain that it would have been useless, that his probing would have been evaded.

George remembers his childhood as being pleasant and uneventful. He felt loved by his mother and enjoyed her bossiness; his father was around most of the time and readily available, as they lived above the store. He was a talkative child who chattered and asked questions endlessly; it was not until he was about six that he noticed that the answers usually came from his mother. His father averted his inquiries either by claiming to be busy or by referring him to his mother.

George did not take this to mean that his father was not interested in him; he merely assumed that his mother knew more. Perhaps mothers were smarter and fathers had to devote themselves to business. His friends confirmed this observation. They said their fathers were hardly ever home, and when they were, they were generally tired and irritable.

His brother, Tom, did not play a significant part during his childhood. He was too old to play with and seemed grumpy most of the time, so George mostly stayed out of his way. He was good at school work and had a lot of friends. He paid no attention to girls.

When he was eleven or so, he began to notice that he liked to watch some of the boys in school while they were running around or playing ball. Their bodies interested him more than the bodies of others and pleased him in a way. One boy in particular drew his attention; he was lean and tall, gentle and yet assured, proud and self-conscious, rugged and yet softly childlike. George discovered with sorrow that he was puny himself; he examined himself before the mirror and his near-sighted eyes, colorless hair, and bony body embarrassed him. He did not feel worthy of Daniel, his ideal.

He tried to lure Daniel away from the other boys and be alone with him. He was willing to do anything to entertain him; he showed him his father's storeroom, bared the secrets of his house, gave him small gifts, and did his homework. One day, Daniel noticed George's favorite book, *War and Peace*, lying on his bedroom table. "It's incomprehensible and boring, isn't it?" he said. George was about to offer an explanation, but bowed his head instead. "It is incomprehensible and boring," he said guiltily. He knew then that he loved Daniel.

Soon after that they began to explore each other's bodies, and spent all their free time together either in Daniel's house or in George's, and one day they were discovered by Tom, who was not supposed to be home at the time. He flew into a rage and beat them severely with his belt. George was so panic-stricken that he did not even feel the pain and he was mortified and ashamed for having exposed Daniel to such humiliation.

Tom reported the incident to their father and George was summoned to the storeroom. His father did not appear to be upset, but he was paler than usual. George was asked what had happened and he freely and ingenuously told his father everything. He had no sense of wrongdoing or guilt, in fact he had no knowledge of homosexuality. He thought it was perfectly natural for him to love Daniel; he saw it as an intensified form of close friendship.

His father listened to him in silence, without interruption. Finally, he spoke, and George remembers every word he said: "It is possible for a male to love another male, I have heard of it. But it is considered wrong and immoral by the world and can only be done in secret. So, let it be your secret and mine and Tom's. Don't ever do it in this house again, and never tell your mother. I am very surprised, but I am not angry. Go now.''

George recalls feeling a wave of gratitude, a tremendous rush of love for his father. He believes that his lack of guilt over his homosexuality is entirely due to his father's reaction, and he modeled his life according to his advice. He continued to meet Daniel, and later others, discreetly, and feels sure that his mother has no inkling of his being gay. He lives in a stable, long-term relationship, far from his hometown, but is in constant touch with his parents. His father has said nothing on the subject of sexuality since the day in the storeroom, when George was thirteen, and has treated him exactly as he had before. Unlike Tom, he has respect for his father's distance; he is in fact grateful for having a father who does not interfere in his life or try to control it.

As for his brother, George has little to say. He can understand his rejection of homosexuality, but not his rage, and he feels hurt because Tom has assiduously avoided introducing him to his wife and will not let him even set eyes on his children. He attributes Tom's anger at their father mainly to insecurity; he feels that Tom is basically unstable, kept afloat by his strong-willed wife.

When George was asked if he thought that his sexual preference was in any way related to his parents, his answer was unhesitatingly negative. He claims they had nothing to do with it at all. He cannot recall even a single moment when he was attracted to a woman, although he likes female company and loves his mother. He has never doubted his masculinity, does not remember any sexual ambiguities, and has always felt perfectly content being himself, without guilt or shame.

It was not easy to induce James, the father, to talk either about himself or his children. He opened up to some extent when he found himself alone with a tape recorder and a bottle of wine. His memories of his father were extremely vague and hazy, and he spoke very hesitantly. He grew up in the South in great poverty, living in a tiny shack with three brothers and his parents. His father worked in a textile mill on the night shift; by the time the children were up, he was already asleep, and they had to keep very quiet until he awakened in the early afternoon. He spent most of his time growing and caring for the vegetables he had planted behind the shack, after which he would go to his favorite tavern for a few beers. In the winter, he went to the tavern right after getting up.

He worked six days a week and slept through most of Sunday. His communication with his family was mainly physical; he beat them frequently and at the slightest provocation. His mother suffered everything silently, and she whacked the boys as well when she was particularly worn out. One by one, the boys left home as soon as they could, without even finishing school; James left when he was thirteen and never went back. He has had no contact with any member of his family since.

He remembers making a decision around the time he was sixteen that his family life was not going to be like his parents'. He promised himself that he would be good to his children, never beat them, always be available to them, and from that time on he worked for that goal single-mindedly. He did not get married until he managed to buy a store of his own, with living quarters above—a proper setting for a proper family life. When Tom was born, he spent more time with the baby than did his mother; he says he was very loving and protective. George was born about five years later, and again he became the main caretaker of the new baby; he now feels he may have begun to neglect Tom because of it.

He admits that he always favored George, but never admitted it even to his wife. George was a happy, healthy baby, a pleasure to take care of, whereas Tom had been choleric and cranky. He maintains his happy disposition to this day, but Tom was always troubled by something. James could never get close to Tom; the boy seemed always to be avoiding him. In contrast, George was always there, "talking a blue streak," helping out without even being asked to. He feels that both boys have turned out well and he has kept the promise he had made to himself. He is sure he did his best and is proud of it.

After he recorded his feelings and memories, he was asked why he had made no mention of George's homosexuality. (He knew that his sons had been interviewed previously.) He said he did not want to take any chances of his wife's overhearing him; otherwise, he claimed not to have any problems about it. He said that George was a sweet boy and seemed happy; that is all that mattered. When he was asked if he regarded himself as distant from his sons, he seemed slightly surprised at the question and thought quite a while before answering. At last, he said he did not think he was. He has always found it difficult to get close to Tom, but as he remembers it, he "watched him closely" while he was growing up and takes credit for getting him interested in becoming an accountant. He believes that Tom is "his own man" and does not want any interference in making decisions; on the other hand, he disapproves of the way Tom is bringing up his children: he interferes with them too much.

As for George, he is quite certain that he was not distant with him. In his recollection, the two of them were always chattering, the boy full of questions, the father full of answers. He feels quite close to him even now, although he only comes home for Christmas. On the whole, now that the subject was brought up, he is sure that he was close to his sons, more to one than to the other, and the fact that they are both happy and successful is the ultimate proof that he must have been a loving father.

One of the most interesting phenomena of family life is the frequently observed tendency of siblings to offer conflicting observations about their parents, both individually and as a couple. The variations are sometimes so pronounced that one is hard put to accept the fact that they are talking about the same person. Perceptions are, of course, always subjective, even when the contemplated object is a tree or a stone. In the case of parents, their behavior is seldom guided by rational, consistently prudent considerations displayed in equal measure to each of their children, and when it is not—which is most of the time—the children view it from separate vantage points. Parental favoritism, which is invariably present in one form or another, never escapes the scrutiny of children, and it is one of the most important factors that determine how they perceive their parents.

In addition to ill-transmitted and ill-received signals between Tom and James, favoritism toward George, clearly observed by all, was a major cause of their lifelong estrangement. Displayed as it was toward a brother who was homosexual made it particularly intolerable to Tom, and he reacted with erratic behavior, designed to attract paternal attention. Deeply resentful toward his father for neglectful and distant behavior, he allayed the guilt he felt by endowing his father with magic powers of sexual potency in his dreams, which in turn interfered with and disturbed his own sexuality.

George's tolerant view of his father's distance is somewhat dubious; it is hard to avoid the suspicion that the tremendous relief he felt at his father's acceptance of his homosexuality caused his overall view of James to turn retroactively roseate. This suspicion is fortified by the fact that he goes home but once a year, even though he lives not far away, and by his admission that he was not interested enough to delve into his father's past to explore the cause of what he called "wounds." The probability is that he was temperamentally—genetically, if you will—better disposed to cope with distant and silent behavior than was Tom.

James's view of his paternal behavior is likely to be somewhat colored by wine, for if his sons agreed on anything at all it was his distance and silence. We must not forget, however, that his own father was absolutely unavailable, except as a source of fear, and compared to that model of fatherhood his behavior toward his sons might justifiably seem warm and close to him.

Paul is an American aristocrat whose family arrived from England in the seventeenth century, already wealthy. By the time he was born before World War I, all matters concerning bringing up children in the family had long become ritualized and routinized. Things were done in a certain way if they were to be done at all, and there was to be no deviation from it, or even discussion of it. True, there had been one or two rebellious ancestors, but nobody got to be notorious, and if there were a few scandals, nothing reached the public eye or ear.

Paul grew up under the stern guidance of his mother and her brother, for his father had been killed in the war before Paul turned ten, and before he could sire the expected number of at least three children. An only child was unheard of in the family, and Paul was brought up with extraordinary care and attention befitting a crown prince. He was tutored privately and extensively until it was time to enter the family's traditional prep school; even there, he had to write a long letter to his mother each day, detailing everything he had done the day before. He also received almost daily letters from home, containing moral advice from his mother and practical counsel from his uncle.

His school years were uneventful and he did well enough to please the family both academically and athletically. Summers were spent traveling with mother and uncle in Europe and he was always kept on an exceedingly short leash. There was no slipping out of hotel rooms after bedtime, no sexual initiation by Continental courtesans or even by chambermaids, but there was a great deal of instruction in matters of obligations, duties, manners, and morals.

College years were not very different. Weekends, which offered the only potential opportunity to break a little loose, had to be spent either visiting mother, a mere two hundred miles away, or being visited. He was the butt of many cruel remarks and jokes by his classmates throughout his college years, but they did not wound Paul. He was well steeped in matters of *noblesse oblige* and endured it all lightly.

Then began the obligatory apprenticeship in the industry that was the centerpiece of the family's holdings, ''starting at the bottom,'' and working his way through all departments of the enterprise, to be installed at the top after twelve to fifteen years of rigorous training. Now a young man in his early twenties, he was permitted, even encouraged, to enter social life with the eventual expectation of finding an appropriate wife. He was still being closely watched, for this was not a family where young men were allowed a period of time when they could indulge themselves in sex or gambling or waiting for chorus girls at stage entrances before devoting themselves to serious matters. This was a family in which moral values were held in the highest regard, higher even than the conduct of business.

Paul was learning his duties both in business and society, and he was having no fun. Looking back on the first twenty-five years of his life now, Paul sees himself as a robot, utterly inexperienced emotionally, growing more and more mechanical with each year, whose only guiding principle was doing one's duty to the family. He is not saying that he was unhappy, for being dutiful can often be intoxicating and being the Sole Male Heir was heady stuff all along. What he regrets in retrospect is the absence of any opportunity for emotional expression, which he sees as a deficit that can never be balanced out.

At the age when he was expected to marry, World War II suspended the rules of the game. Being thirty-two and an executive in an essential war industry, he would normally have been exempted, but he insisted on getting a commission, acting against the interests of the family for the first time in his life. He argued that if duty was regarded as the highest principle of conduct; then duty to one's country must be the highest of duties. He went off to war in 1942.

He had a quiet war aboard naval supply ships, but he saw many things he would never have seen otherwise, and mingled with people he would never have met. He even got involved in a number of squalid sexual scrapes, which he found distasteful and caused serious concern for the future. Was it always going to be like that? And if so, how can marriage be tolerable? There was no one with whom he could discuss the problem.

He came home and resumed his duties, but it was not the same. He was restless and found his old environment, his

old friends, boring. He began to suspect that there was a
darker side to his nature, and to allay his fears he soon married a young socialite, ten years his junior. Her status and
money were appropriate to his station, and although he
found his fears about sex to be confirmed, they had two children before sexual activity came to an end between them.

Their son, David, is now thirty-four, their daughter, Isabel,
twenty-seven. Their perceptions of their father are strikingly
different, as are his of them. David feels that he is primarily his
father's ego extension, his surrogate for living; he is afraid that
his father has overinvested in him emotionally and in terms of
expectations and that both of them are heading for an emotional
crisis. Isabel, on the other hand, sees her father as icily distant
and hopelessly silent, and claims that he has probably ruined
her life. They agree that nothing could be expected of their
mother, whose energies were devoted to keeping her affairs
discreet when they were children and who is now absorbed in
patronizing young artists.

By David's account, his upbringing was closely overseen
by his father and followed the traditions of the family. He
felt that while Paul was strict, there was an aura of apology
about him. When he was entered in prep school and college,
his father seemed to be saying that he was sorry for making
David do these things, but they could not be helped. He was
kept closely at bay in matters affecting education and family, but his father counseled him confidentially to enjoy himself otherwise. This was strictly between the two of them, to
be kept secret from others.

At first, David found the arrangement satisfactory, but he
soon discovered that he was doing his father's bidding most
of the time. He would be told, for example, to go to a
specified bar or hotel lounge, often a seedy one, pick up a
woman and take her to a motel, also specified. He would
then be questioned closely by Paul on every detail and
praised for his efforts. Whenever David reported that his
sexual experience was satisfying or pleasurable, his father
seemed incredulous. He made him repeat it and shook his
head in puzzlement or disbelief.

He was also instructed to see certain movies and plays and

furnish extensive reports, or to date certain young women of good social standing and go as far with them sexually as he could. His father was especially interested in that. When David reported success for the majority of these dates, Paul seemed positively shaken. It appeared to the son that his father was unable to accept the possibility of sexual pleasure and shrank from the discovery that young women from irreproachable families seldom needed too much persuasion to have sex.

David admits to a lack of willpower. While it did not take him long to realize that what his father was doing, using him for a stand-in, was wrong, he found himself helpless. In families like David's, all matters are regarded as either morally right or morally wrong, and words like "neurotic" are never used, thereby foreclosing intervention from sources that are readily available to others. Psychoanalysis and psychotherapy are still considered radical procedures and are resorted to only in extreme circumstances. Thus, David was in a bind from which he could not extricate himself without help. He thought of discussing the situation with his friends, but dismissed the notion; it was not something one could talk about with friends. He approached his sister, but as soon as she found that he wanted to talk about their father, she cut him off curtly with the statement, "Father is a creepy bastard and I don't want to discuss anything about him."

Meanwhile, Paul was also pressing David in his career. Installed in the family enterprise after college, he was being pushed through much too fast, David felt. He was made executive vice-president at twenty-eight to the chagrin of senior executives, and his father kept thrusting added responsibilities at him, burdening him beyond the limits of his endurance. Paul constantly instructed him to expand, to invest, to reorganize, to hire, to fire, until one day David was overcome and suffered a major nervous breakdown.

He was found in a motel room, unconscious, with a needle mark on his arm; he was apparently introduced to heroin by a pickup he had taken to the motel. In strict secrecy, he was taken to an exclusive sanatorium; only members of the immediate family were told about it; all others were told he was on an extended business trip abroad. According to the psychiatrist who attended him, David was suffering from nervous exhaustion brought on by extreme stress. Later, he was diagnosed as a schizoid personality by another psychiatrist, and as suffering from extremely defective self-image by a third.

David's recovery was uncomplicated, but intensive psychotherapy was recommended and David has been participating in it for two years now. He has gained insight, yet he is not optimistic about the future. He has learned, as he had already suspected, that he has been the subject of his father's ego extension all his life; through him, Paul experienced vicariously all that had been denied to himself in his youth and which he was temperamentally unable to attain for himself in his maturity. David feels that his father has been unscrupulous in using his son as an intermediary between himself and those aspects of life that he was incapable of utilizing and exploring himself, especially sex. He is specifically bitter because he has lost the pleasure of sexual activity—one of the prices he paid for his new insights. He now feels that his father is peering over his shoulders while he is having sex, which robs him of his pleasure and is slowly but surely alienating him from sex altogether. He has no steady relationships and does not expect to marry. He picks up women occasionally in the same places he was originally directed to by his father.

David is back at work with a reduced range of responsibilities; his father, still very much in charge, was strongly advised to relieve him of many of his former duties. David believes that Paul suffered a grave shock when his son had a breakdown for at least two reasons: for one, nervous breakdowns were unprecedented in the family's history, and for another, he has lost his emissary to the forbidden world. Nevertheless, he expects Paul to "move in on" him soon once again; he has invested himself so heavily in his son that he will not be able to write it off.

David is very sad—not depressed, he emphasizes, but sad—at thirty-four. He admits freely that he is not strong.

He is well educated and good at his work, but beyond these assets he feels undeveloped. His "persona is empty," he says; his father can seduce and seize it again at will.

David's sister Isabel is an extraordinarily attractive woman of twenty-seven, an internationally known painter who has exhibited in half a dozen countries and received respectful reviews. Her earnings from her work are considerable, and she uses her very substantial income from family trusts to support young painters who have not had successes yet. She is quick-witted, was educated at the best finishing schools and colleges in the United States and France, is versatile in a number of languages, a stimulating conversationalist—to all appearances a veritable gem. Isabel also hates men and misses no opportunity to demean, mistreat, and humiliate them, although she is completely heterosexual.

She attributes her unconcealed venom at men entirely to her father's treatment of her, which she can never forgive. The reason she gives for her determined unforgivingness is that she is terribly unhappy about her feelings toward men. She would like to have normal relations with them, she would like to be able to marry and have children, she would like to stop abusing them—but she is unable to make a move in that direction. She has had several attempts at various forms of therapy, including orthodox analysis, but found that therapists were "too slow." Besides, she has delved deeply into the literature and believes that she can anticipate therapeutic opinions; since she knows the underlying causes of her condition, she does not need diagnosis or prognosis. She needs some form of as yet undiscovered help in recovering from her malignant state, but does not expect to find it, not while her father is alive at any rate.

Isabel's feelings do not extend to her mother, whom she dismisses as being "simple"—a woman who loves tiny babies but does not know, or claim to know, what to do with them after they outgrow her arms. She had very little role in Isabel's upbringing, and she remembers very little about her mother before age six or so. She does, however, remember her father very well from the time she was in her playpen.

He would come to her room each day and watch her play for what seemed like a long time; sometimes he would talk to her, but she could not understand.

Then, suddenly, he vanished from Isabel's life. She did not know what had happened until much later: David entered boarding school, his education began, and it required his father's full attention. Girls were of secondary importance anyway in the family tradition unless they were an only child; they were to be brought up and married off properly; they were to cause no problems. No woman in the family has ever had an independent career.

Tradition aside, Isabel took her father's disappearance as an insult to herself. This man who came to see her every day and talk to her and watch her play did not come anymore. Whenever she asked her nanny or mother where he was, she would be told that he was busy, he was with brother David. To Isabel, he has made a choice between her and her brother; he has chosen David and rejected her.

It was then that she began to draw pictures. At first, they were all images of her father, not at all childlike squiggles but realistic renderings, and she would tape them to the walls of her room. This was tolerated by the nanny for a while, but one day they were all gone; nice girls did not plaster their walls with drawings. From then on, the pictures, drawn and immediately discarded, became less and less realistic and soon turned into abstract compositions. Through art, Isabel was expelling her father from her consciousness.

Unlike her brother, Isabel was exceptionally strong-willed and independent-minded. She was not going to cry because daddy was not visiting her anymore, she was not going to whine and carry on; she was going to do without him, proudly. She saw him only at Sunday breakfasts during that period and willfully avoided looking at him; if he addressed her, she replied without turning her head, and when he occasionally tried to touch her, she would slip away. If he noticed the change in her, he did not say anything about it.

Throughout her school years, Isabel was consumed with study and art. She was always at the top of her class, and her art work, now watercolors and oils, was often displayed in assembly halls and teachers' offices. When she was home for vacations and family occasions, she was polite and proper to everyone, including her father, and she often heard relatives remark how "exquisite" she was. At school, she formed many close friendships, and some of the girls remained friends to this day. Boys were not an issue until she entered college, for her previous schools were for girls only.

Her college years proved to be the beginning of an ever-increasingly painful period in her life; she had to learn to cope with boys and learn how she felt about them. She had never had an unchaperoned date before, hardly ever thought about boys, and never listened to the whisperings and giggles of her schoolmates. Her mother, who should have traditionally instructed her on all matters relating to boys, was fully occupied with her own affairs, and no one else thought to do anything about it. Consequently, Isabel had no script for dealing with boys; she had to make it up as she went along, existentially.

She attracted boys in droves, which confused her at first, and she dealt with it by turning them all away and concentrating on studies and art. Even so, for the first time in her life, the palpable presence of males all around her did something to her, releasing previously unthought thoughts, unfelt feelings, ancient angers. On the intellectual level, she was perfectly familiar with anatomy and biology, and she had even studied sex manuals, but now the repressions came to the fore—she started dreaming about her father and fantasizing about him and other faceless men. It was during her freshman year that she had her first dream about her father, a dream that was to remain recurrent to the present. She saw her father lying naked on a slab of stone or marble, as if he were dead, his penis erect. It was like a photograph; everything was still and unmoving, black and white, a medium shot.

For a while, the dream also appeared as a fantasy, flashing on unexpectedly like a slide, soon to be replaced by more vivid tableaux. She would then try to mount her prone father, but his figure was made of some cold, hard, slippery

42

material, and she would slide off him helplessly. Her hands would attempt to get a hold on his penis for leverage, but that too was waxy, unsupporting, and she would crumble on the cold floor. The fantasy would seize her unpredictably, while she was reading a book, or walking to class, or watching a boring movie. Unlike the original dream, this fantasy presented itself in full color and in varying perspectives; sometimes her father's body would be lying at an angle, not horizontally, or, very rarely, it would be standing like a statue. She hated that, because she would slide off him and fall as if from a great height.

She always felt anger after these fantasies—an unfocused, self-breeding anger—and she had to throw herself into some activity to shake it off. At times, she tried to alter the fantasy by replacing her father's body with another, but it would dissolve before she could even touch it. She undertook Freudian analysis at this point, but she already knew the texts, and the analyst was silent. She gave it up after a couple of months.

Her first date took place toward the end of her freshman year. She chose him on the basis of physical appeal and because he was her most ardent pursuer. They went to a movie on a Sunday afternoon and he did not try to hold hands. At dinner, he was mannerly but boring. He did not seem to know much about anything except geodesic domes, and she wished to be elsewhere, alone. He took her back to her apartment and wanted to come in, but she said no. When he tried to kiss her, she averted her mouth.

He continued to pursue her and she let him take her out several times without rewarding him for his constancy, not out of design or cruelty as yet, but for lack of desire and decision. She was also beginning to experience a new, triumphant feeling of power: His future course with her was entirely in her hands, he was in her charge.

After about a month of persistent pursuit, she decided to satisfy her curiosity and allowed him to try to make love to her. To her surprise, she was quickly inflamed, and to her greater surprise, she found herself dominating him. Despite his muscular strength, it was she who guided him from one step to another, and he followed her totally. Then, as she was about to mount him at the height of her passion, his excitement exploded him, and to her horror he was suddenly slippery like her fantasized father. She slid off and screamed at him to get out. She stayed up all night for fear of dreaming.

She spent that summer in Europe with a girlfriend and devoted herself entirely to picking up men. She would string them along as long as possible, satisfy her passion, and then order them out. She never allowed one to spend the night, and so strong was her power over men that even the rough ones who were used to women doing their bidding deferred to her like sheep. By the time she came back to college, she was certain that she despised men, that she would use and abuse them all her life; they were going to pay for the sins of her father.

She manipulates men into intricate dependency relationships, forces them into passive, masochistic roles sexually, and demeans them in as many ways as possible. All this gives her passionate pleasure, but she remains angry because it cannot be otherwise; she is impatiently waiting for her father to die, hoping that it might effect a change.

She feels sorry for her brother for being so weak, for allowing his father to "vampirize" him. She thinks the only thing that can save him is marriage to a woman of strong will who would shield him from his father's incursions.

Paul, who spoke freely of his life before his marriage, is not very forthcoming on the subject of his children. He does feel sorry, even guilty, about what happened to David, but at the same time he cannot conceal his disappointment about his lack of strength and "solidity." He realizes now that times have changed since his own youth, and that perhaps he should not have forced David into a pattern of upbringing that may be obsolete. He claims he did it reluctantly, but could not think of another way.

He was even more reluctant to talk about Isabel, although he called her "a splendid creature." He said he was not prepared for bringing up a daughter, nor was his wife. He simply did not know what to do with her, how to behave, what to say. He claimed that he tried to get close to her when she was little, but it felt somehow strange; "women really are quite different from us." He professed to admire Isabel and wished that things could be different. Again, he did not know how.

In light of his overwhelming attention to his son and his cold distance from his daughter, he was asked, should one assume that he favored the former? Not at all, he said. In fact, he favored Isabel—if only she could be his son, and David his daughter . . .

The interrelationships of Paul, David, and Isabel could provide material for several novels, but for our narrower purposes they dramatize how a father can be distant to one child and overwhelmingly obtrusive to another. One suspects that Paul's choice was guided principally by gender; he could not have possibly acted otherwise toward a son, nor a daughter. His own childhood and youth were characterized by virtual sensory deprivation and the absence of a father figure; so arid was his life that having a son must have seemed to him like salvation. He could now breathe and act out his fantasies through his son, his ambassador to the unexplored world. Isabel, on the other hand, belonged to the barren side of his life. He had no capacity to enjoy women in any sense, and having a daughter was embarrassing and painful.

Ironically, he was to be chagrined by the weakness and failure of the son and the strength and success of the daughter, but there is no evidence that he is aware of his crucial role in the outcome. He is capable of seeing them for what they are, but he is unable to alter his behavior toward them; it is almost certain that he will continue to "vampirize" his son and remain withdrawn from his daughter.

True to character, David reacted negatively by means of a nervous breakdown whereas Isabel responded actively both in fantasy and real life. Her rage, repressed in her day-to-day existence, came to the fore in her dreams and fantasies, to be acted out later in her vengeful treatment of men. She is the true object of our sympathy because she lost more than the other two. Paul and David were deprived of many experiences only because they lacked the strength of character to lunge for them; Isabel is deprived of what she wants most not by weakness but the paralyzing silence of her father.

seductive

Geoffrey is a lawyer in an industrial city in the Midwest. He is forty-two, a short, balding man with warm brown eyes, thoughtful, funny, introspective. By choice, his practice is focused on working-class clients and consists mainly of cases of accidents, compensation, real estate, and insurance. Geoffrey's father had been a Communist, very active through the socially turbulent 1930s, a volunteer in Spain, mostly absent on Communist party business, but very affectionate when home—a "wonderful, sweet father" to Geoffrey.

Although disenchanted with the party after the Soviet-Nazi pact, the father's social and economic views remained on the radical side and he instilled in Geoffrey an acute social conscience. He always wanted his son to become a union organizer, but when Geoffrey opted for law, he was delighted. He was always very supportive to his son and gentle to his wife, although his long absences took their toll on family life and the mother was always the main wage earner.

The McCarthy era ruined his father's already limited

earning powers, and Geoffrey had to work in after-school jobs through high school and support himself throughout college and law school. He did not mind it at all, although he did not like seeing his mother working hard all the time. Still, he never blamed his father for their needy conditions for everyone in the family believed that ideals were more important than anything.

Geoffrey's parents live in Florida now, their Social Security income supplemented by his gifts of money. It is apparent that he loves them dearly; his eyes often turn moist when he talks about his father's exploits in Spain, his organizing work during World War II, and his unjust sufferings at the hands of McCarthy's minions. He has great respect for his mother for enduring all those years with hardly a complaint.

He married a young woman of his age while still in law school; she had had a previous bitterly brief marriage and she was the first woman Geoffrey ever fell in love with. He has never wavered in his affections, and his wife, Susan, appears to be totally devoted to him. If he has any gripe with life at all, it is the way his law practice has turned out. Originally, he entered the profession in order to help the poor, but he was soon to find that lawyering was not the best approach to that area. He had thought of going to work for a welfare agency or something comparable, but the pay was unacceptably low. Their daughter, Sarah, was born a year after their marriage, followed three years later by a son, Jim, and he was acutely aware of his responsibilities as family man. In that one respect, he did not want to follow his father's example.

He had to settle for the kind of law practice that served some of the needs of the working class, if not of the poor, and compensates for his disappointment by serving as court-appointed attorney as often as he can afford to. He hopes that at least one of his children will follow the pattern he originally set for himself, although prospects are not promising at the moment. Sarah, at twenty, is going through a "rebellious phase," steadfastly refusing to go to college, and Jim, at seventeen, does not show much motivation or enthusiasm for anything yet. It is too soon to tell, but Geoffrey is optimistic by nature.

Sarah moved away from home after graduating from high school and now lives in a metropolitan area in the East. She has a bare studio apartment and pays her expenses any way she can. She works as a waitress for a while, or saleswoman, or photographer's model; sometimes she ''borrows'' money from men with no intention of paying them back. She also gets a monthly allowance from her father, but without the knowledge of her mother.

Sarah is not attractive, yet she always has lots of men around; they seem to like her provocative manners, her sexual suggestiveness. She has a reputation of being athletic and exotic in bed, and she is clearly proud of it. She has constant crushes and is forever trying to get married men to leave their wives for her. She likes sex best under dangerous and extreme circumstances, ''scrapes,'' as she calls them, such as performing fellatio in a car while the man is driving, or in a bathroom during a party with somebody's husband. Her first sexual experience took place in the boys' shower while a gym class was in progress.

Her plans for the future are vague. She does not intend to go to college for any reason, but she is a voracious reader and has an excellent grasp of world literature. Some thought has been given to a career in writing, for which she claims to have a knack. She has written stories and shows them to friends, but never tried to sell one.

Marriage does not have a large part in Sarah's plans; she does not think she will marry, but definitely wants a baby when she is around thirty. Men, on the other hand, do have a leading role; she says she loves them, in and out of bed, and has great ambitions in that regard. She wants to become mistress of the great men of our times, and Alma Mahler and Lou Andreas Salome are her heroines. She trains for her role by keeping copious notebooks filled with witty quotes, which she commits to memory and uses at every opportunity without attribution. If she gets caught, she will say, ''I took it for granted that you knew that.'' She is very good at this, and one can see the allure of her façade.

It was quite difficult to get her to speak about her childhood, her father, her past, because her interest in the present and future is much greater; even while she talks, her eyes are roving and one can see that she is thinking of something else. When she is finally persuaded to look back, her tone is offhanded and patronizing.

She began by calling her mother a "bitch and a harpy," and holds her solely responsible for having left home at seventeen. She is convinced that Sue, as she calls her, holds her father in the palm of her hand and controls everything he does outside his professional activities. Her other villain is Geoffrey's father, whom she blames for Geoffrey's "lowlife" legal practice. She thinks the old man is a bombastic ideologue and that he tried to shape his son in his image and largely succeeded, despite his long absences from home. The only difference between the two, as she perceives it, is that ideals men could once believe in and die for, right or wrong, are gone, passé, and Geoffrey had found himself trained to be an idealist with no ideals. (Using foreign and quasi-foreign words liberally, she called him an idealist *manqué* several times.) Her father could have been a successful corporation or tax lawyer, she believes, had it not been for the old man's glorification of the poor. Sarah herself has no use for the poor.

When her attention is called to her present way of life, which is not significantly different from poverty as she has almost no furniture, barely enough clothes, and nothing for luxuries, she emphasizes that she is passing through the "early romantic" phase of her life where money is regarded casually. She does, however, have an important role reserved for money in her future; after she will have had her baby, money will be essential in great quantity, for she will be devoting herself entirely to rearing him to be a great man. Her plans do not include a daughter.

According to Sarah, the children were told at an early age by their mother—Jim later confirmed this—that "father came first" in all matters relating to the family. His well-being had precedence over everything else because he was sickly and needed constant care. (He never made any reference to illness in our talks.) The mother was to be the intermediary between children and father, and while they saw him at dinner every night, they were not supposed to bother him with anything that resembled a problem.

Nevertheless, behind mother's back, father and daughter formed a special relationship that was very exciting to Sarah. He would get out of bed after Susan was asleep and go to Sarah's room and gently awaken her. These nightly visits began when Sarah was very young, perhaps four, and continued until she left home. He would sit on the edge of her bed, hold her hand, and talk to her. At first, until she was eight or so, he would read her a story and then talk to her about anything that came to her mind. As she grew older, the visits consisted of his listening to Sarah's troubles, her complaints about her mother, her school life, and counseling her on all her problems. They both spoke in whispered tones, thereby adding to the excitement of their conspiracy, and before leaving he would say, "Remember, this is our secret."

They were caught by mother only once during these years, but Geoffrey said he could not sleep, decided to look in on Sarah, and found her awake. She accepted the explanation and they were not discovered again.

The excitement of their meetings carried over into Sarah's days. She often planned what she was going to tell him that night while her attention wandered at school or while she was riding the school bus home. At dinner, they exchanged secret glances and winks when no one was looking. When Sarah began fantasizing at thirteen, father was the principal player; the fantasies were often, not always, sexual, and revolved around the theme of his staying with her all night and being found in the morning by mother.

The excitement sustained itself to the end, but during the last few years Sarah often found herself angry at him. Why did he have to keep their meetings from mother? Was he afraid of her? Why did he not confront her and announce that he was going to visit his daughter every night, and that is how it was going to be!? Was he weak? Were all men weak?

She decided to find out, and her sexual experimentations began before she was sixteen. She found that men did seem to be weak, at least in regard to her; more than one boy broke up with his steady girl for Sarah's favors. Increasingly, she pressed Geoffrey on the subject of mother and plagued him with questions, but he remained evasive and sheepish on the subject. Another subject that was taboo to him was dating or anything having to do with boys. She tried to talk to him about it, but he shut her off. He told Sarah to discuss these matters with her mother only.

Mother was extremely prudish about sex; she was constantly cautioning Sarah on the subject of "going too far" with boys, and used words and phrases remembered from her teens, such as "petting" or "necking," words nobody used anymore. Sarah could not take her seriously on the subject, and as she was nearing graduation, she decided to bring matters out into the open. She had known that mother was in the habit of going through her drawers and closet, looking for something incriminating, and having just read *Goodbye, Columbus*, she placed her diaphragm where her mother could easily find it, which she did almost immediately. The scene Sarah had anticipated took place exactly as imagined; she was called a number of names and threatened with all sorts of vague disasters that would overtake her if she did not behave like a "nice girl."

A few days later, Geoffrey suffered a heart attack, and coming home from the hospital on the first day of his stay, mother turned on daughter in an uncontrollable rage. She accused Sarah of being directly responsible for her father's condition: "You are going to kill him, you little slut!" she screamed. When Sarah defended herself by saying that father knew nothing about her diaphragm, Susan seized her by the throat and hissed, "I told him. I wanted him to know what kind of daughter he had!"

Sarah was extremely shaken by that confrontation. Her feelings toward father turned bitter; she regarded his heart attack as a failure of heart, a loss of courage. If only he had asserted himself, she thought, it would not have happened. She stopped talking to her mother during Geoffrey's recovery, which was swift and uncomplicated, and avoided his eyes when she was with him. On the first day he went back to work, Susan packed a few things and left home.

After a couple of months in the East, Sarah wrote her father at his office. It was a stiff, formal letter, without apologies, but he answered and enclosed a check. They do correspond about once a month, but their letters are merely newsy and lack exchanges of affection. Mother is not mentioned by either, and Sarah has been out of touch with her since she left home.

When she is asked how she feels about her nightly rendezvous with father now, she is hesitant. She is quite aware that her compulsion to try to get men to leave their wives for her is rooted in their conspiracy, yet she is not sure whether to look upon it as a psychological failing or a "romantic tendency." She is free of guilt feelings and does not think she will change; at least not until she has had her baby boy.

Geoffrey is fine now and will talk freely about his work and home life. There are only two subjects that never come up: his health and his nightly visits in Sarah's room. As for Jim, he declines to talk about his parents and thinks Sarah is "swell."

The seductive father, like the distant one, tends to have a strong impact on the sexuality of his daughter. Sarah resembles Isabel in the sense that they are both hostile to men, even though their hostility is expressed in different forms. Isabel plays out hers by demeaning and humiliating them whereas Sarah acts more deviously, by prying on their weaknesses. They both exploit men, but Isabel's methods are direct and simple, and Sarah's contrived, far-ranging.

Sarah's hostility, unlike Isabel's, stems from her perception that men are weak. Her father, certainly, is weak—he has to sneak around to be with his daughter, he is submissive to his wife, as he was to his father; he even has a heart attack, the most dramatic show of weakness for Sarah. Their nightly meetings were exciting for her, and the flame they lit is still burning, but their concealment, their secret, was the product of weakness. It said to her that men had to be taken in hand, they had to come to her in defiance of their wives. The one who came and stayed would redeem the others.

Sarah's situation is aggravated by two additional factors. There is a genuine generational gap separating her from her father; he and his father belong to a world that is no longer discernible to her. Also, and more seriously, her mother made her feel unwanted and guilty, generating and reinforcing her belief in the superior strength of women.

Anthony is a film producer who admits to being forty-seven. He is exceptionally handsome and glamorous, dresses in the latest California style, and is immaculately groomed from haircut to prescribed shoes. He is verbose but not mindless, glib but not shallow. He has been married a number of times and he is almost constantly on the way to somewhere, accompanied by one aspiring actress or another. He pays several alimonies, but has only one child from his first marriage—Meg, now twenty-five.

He grew up in a teeming near-slum of a metropolitan area, the only child of an immigrant shoemaker from a Mediterranean country. His mother worked as a seamstress whenever she could find work, and the boy was often left to his own devices. He was never neglected, though; he always had clean clothes and good shoes and enough to eat. His needs came first in the family, and if there was one portion of ice cream for dessert, Anthony was the one to get it. He also received detailed daily instructions from his mother when she was working; she had to be told in advance where he would be every minute of the day. His father was very strict and quick with both hands; he could slap the boy with either at an alarming speed.

He was not cruel, though, and never punished Anthony without reason. Rules of conduct were established, covering every phase of his daily life; only breaching the rules brought retribution. His mother spoiled him with sweets whenever she could afford it; all he ever got from his father was a constant flow of advice. There seemed to be no imaginable contingency in life that he could not explain or illuminate with a folk saying, and by the time the boy was six he began wondering why his father was a shoemaker. He envisioned him sitting in a palatial room, surrounded by disciples, and receiving bearers of problems. He would listen, nod, and supply the solution, ready for the next supplicant.

Anthony behaved himself and gave his parents little to worry about. He stayed out of trouble but had many opportunities to observe it in the streets; he learned about petty crimes, street fights, illicit dealings, and, most importantly, poverty. Many of his friends had not enough to eat and holes in their shoes, and Anthony was determined at a very young age not to be poor, ever. Everybody kept telling him how handsome he was, and he established a link in his mind between being handsome and not being poor, though he did not know what that might be.

He got good grades in school and managed to gain admission to an excellent high school. It was there that he found the link when he was asked to join the drama club: being handsome meant that it would be easy to become an actor, maybe even a movie star. When he told his mother about his newly found ambition, she was happy and encouraging. His father thought he was a fool. He stood in front of the mirror and made grotesque faces; "See that?" he asked, "anybody can be an actor. You need a good trade or else you will starve. Acting is for sissies."

Anthony was keenly disappointed in his father's reaction and did not confide in him after that episode. He worked hard with the drama club and soon became a star performer, but shared the news with his mother only. At about the same time, he began to discover that handsomeness offered other advantages as well—he began to discover women. He knew all about them, he thought at the time; there was a lot of talk in the streets about them, a mixture of bragging, half-truths, and hard facts. "They all want the same thing," was the general consensus, and Anthony had no reason to disbelieve it. They certainly wanted him, one way or another, and there was much groping and fumbling in dark corners, stairways, and the occasional luxury of back seats.

When he graduated in the late 1940s, he had yet to spend a night with a woman. At a time when the Pill was far in the future and abortion only whispered about, sex was an uncertain, sometimes dangerous, endeavor. To be found by a girl's father in a compromising position was equated with instant death, and going to prostitutes was financially prohibitive. He did know one thing for certain, though; he knew that he loved women and the things they could do to a man, and he was determined to have as many of them as he could manage in a lifetime.

He started making the rounds at theatrical agents and casting offices right after graduation while supporting himself with a job at a supermarket. He was still living at home under his father's glare and the beaming of his mother, saving his money for a ticket to Hollywood. And, as luck would have it, there was great demand for Latin good looks at the time, and Anthony found himself in Hollywood for screen tests three months after graduation.

He got small parts, met Doris, an established costume designer, and spent his first night in bed with a woman at last. He liked it so much that without giving it a thought he married her. It did cross his mind, he admits today, that her steady and adequate income would come in handy between parts. And parts were scarce; it seems that Anthony's looks were not supplemented by sufficient talent, and soon most of his jobs were as an extra.

He does not remember whether it was disappointment in his career or his natural love of women that compelled him to become a full-time womanizer; it may have been a combination of both. In any case, he had a lot of quick affairs, especially after Doris became pregnant—an unplanned event. Even more unplanned was Doris's discovery of his activities; a friend of theirs told her all about it in the maternity ward, a couple of days after she gave birth to Meg.

Doris filed for divorce immediately, locked him out of the house, and kept him from seeing Meg. He was jobless, penniless, and homeless when he met a woman who worked in film editing and she told him there was more future in production work than in acting. He followed the advice and soon had a steady job. For the first time, he was able to send some money to his mother and write his father about his exaggeratedly prosperous new existence. If only he could have visited Meg regularly, he would have been quite content.

It took Doris and Anthony three years to reach a reasonable divorce agreement, and by that time he was a successful producer for a major studio. He will never forget the day when he was to see his daughter for the first time. He could not sleep the night before and did not play his customary eighteen holes of Sunday morning golf with his new wife. He spent the morning primping in front of the mirror, wondering what his daughter would think of the way he looked. He shaved twice and chose his clothes with even more care than he usually did; he noticed that his hands were trembling.

He arrived at Doris's house in a chauffeur-driven studio limousine at exactly one o'clock and rang the bell. The housekeeper pointed him toward the living room where Doris stood, as if posing for a photograph, holding the hand of a little girl in a pink dress. "This is your daughter, Meg," she said, "Meg, this is your father," and left the room. The little girl seemed scared to death and he was on the verge of tears. He will remember this tableau forever, but he cannot remember the rest of the day.

Eventually, it was so arranged that Meg would spend her weekends and one month in the summer with her father. Anthony's eyes gleam as he describes the wonderful times the two of them had together. He would take her to zoos and Disneyland and ball games, and teach her to play golf. He would read her stories and shower her with expensive gifts; in the summer, he would take her traveling, to the Grand Canyon, to Niagara Falls, to Europe. When he is asked how all this fitted into his grueling schedule, he pauses and says that sometimes he could not be there, but his wife and Meg got along wonderfully well.

By the time Meg was in her early teens, Anthony was enormously successful and sent her to the most fashionable school in Switzerland. As he recalls it, once a month or so he would visit her, no matter what part of the world he was working in, and his visits became a treat for the whole school. He would arrive from Zurich airport in a private plane laden with gifts for students and teachers, most of whom had a crush on Meg's wonderful, handsome father. During summer vacations, she would spend a month at her father's elegant estate in the hills, now presided over by still another new wife. Anthony says they got along splendidly.

Anthony says that the years in Switzerland represented the "honeymoon" phase in his relationship with Meg. He claims she changed while she was in college, turned a little remote and hostile. He thinks she may have been experimenting with drugs. She no longer wanted to spend part of her summer vacations with him, she preferred backpacking with friends in the Rockies or the Alps. He was still in the habit of sending her all sorts of extravagant gifts, but she no longer seemed excited over them and rarely sent a thank-you note.

After she finished college, Meg refused his offer of a choice of jobs in the film business, but she felt she had to sort things out before deciding on anything. Next he heard from her, she was in a Zen retreat in the East and planned to remain there at least a year. Anthony did not understand; he asked Doris and she assured him that Meg was a very sensible girl and should be trusted to know what is best for her.

She did stay at the retreat for over a year and did not get in touch with her father until several months later. She wrote him that she had an interesting job with a small magazine that did a lot of investigatory journalism and asked him not to send her money or gifts any longer. She had everything she wanted.

He flew up to see her uninvited and found that the "small magazine" was in fact run from one room in a shabby house and that Meg was living in a commune-type arrangement with half a dozen men and women of assorted ages. She was very cool to him and seemed embarrassed by him when he asked to be introduced to her friends. She made him promise not to visit her again uninvited, and gently but firmly asked him not to get in touch with her without hearing from her first.

It has been over a year now that Anthony last saw his daughter, and he does not understand what has happened. His parents have died and Meg is his only family now; he is deeply hurt and does not know what to do. Doris thinks Meg will "come out of it all right." Anthony's analyst says she may or may not.

Meg is almost painfully thin and pays no attention to her appearance, yet she has obviously inherited her father's striking features. It would take little effort to turn her into an attractive young woman. She speaks slowly as if she had written down each sentence before she spoke it. She is very calm and relaxed without visible nervous habits. Living in a Zen community seems to agree with her; in fact, she plans to stay for the rest of her life.

She talks about her father freely, like someone who has thought a great deal about the subject she speaks of. The moment so cherished by her father when he first set eyes on his daughter is unremembered by her. Her first memory of him is sitting on his lap in the back seat of a very large car while he was talking to someone on the telephone. She remembers the house he used to live in with his second wife who, Meg thought, was extremely affectionate with her. In her memory, he was seldom home during the weekends she was visiting him, but when he was, they had a lot of fun. He had a habit of tickling her, which she loved more than anything. She recalls a trip to New York particularly well because he had a strange woman meet them at the airport who was introduced to her as Aunt Maggie. She was staying in the same hotel, adjacent to their suite. She was very proud of her father, because people seemed to stare at him a lot in public places and everyone they met was especially nice to her. She also loved all the presents he gave her, because that showed how much he loved her.

Having to go to Switzerland made her very sad. That wonderful, handsome man, her father, who showered her with presents like a suitor, was no longer near. He did call her about twice a month, and came to visit her at the school twice every year she was there, flying in like an eagle, with gifts for everyone. It made her jealous that all the other girls and the younger woman teachers treated him so warmly. When she was asked if she was certain about the frequency of his visits, she said she used to keep a diary that listed every time she saw him—a total of seven times in four years. During her first summer vacation, she was deeply hurt when she found a different wife greeting her. They had just married, and he seemed to pay more attention to the new wife than to Meg. She recognized for the first time that her father was inconstant; no woman, including herself, could count on his continuing presence.

She was a young woman by then, fourteen or fifteen, and should have begun to be interested in boys. When she returned for her second year in Switzerland, she found that all the other girls in her class had had some sort of experience with boys during the summer. She made up a story when it was her turn to report, something she had seen her father and his new wife do in the swimming pool. She felt that her father had spoiled other men for her, seduced her. He was so beautiful, so powerful, so generous . . . How could she become interested in anyone else?

Meg blames her father for her stifled sexuality. The weekends, the gifts, the travels—everything combined to turn him into a knight and her into his lady. She winced at the memory of his looking around furtively before sneaking into a young music teacher's room during his last visit to her school, unaware that he was observed by Meg and her best friend. She was mortified but her friend comforted her and promised not to tell anyone.

That scene became the foundation of all her fantasies; they all began with the moment when he entered the teacher's room, and she played out endless variations on what must have taken place behind that door. The opening of the door was the most erotic scene she has ever witnessed.

During college, she attempted to overcome the arid state she was in by dating a lot of boys, but nothing came of it; she just could not get interested and felt no passion stirring. Then she happened upon Zen Buddhism while walking by a bookshelf and found it to be soothing—a balm to her tortured spirit. The rest followed naturally and she arrived at where she is now. She has never had any sort of sexual experience, except for the pressing of a few mouths on her cold lips, and desires none. Everyone in her community lives contented lives of celibate devotion to the spirit of Zen, and Meg feels she could not attain anything higher.

Anthony's seductiveness was very different from Geoffrey's. It did not have the quality of secretiveness and danger; instead, it had enchantment and glamour. Its effect on Meg was also quite different; instead of promiscuity and exploitation of men, it brought her chastity, the deliberate rejection of the sexual aspect of men and women.

Anthony discovered the fruits of seductiveness early in life. It was the most advantageous approach to women, as well as his passport away from the shoemaker's shop. It worked with every woman he met, it worked with Doris, and when the time came to act as a father, he had no other resource. He was a deliberate, conscious seducer—unlike Geoffrey, a guileless, ingenuous one—and he had all sorts of props at hand to aid him. It did not take much to enchant a little girl, but the props came in handy when the state of enchantment had to be maintained at a distance.

It is difficult to say whether Anthony is dishonest or self-deceptive when he greatly exaggerates the frequency of his presence in Meg's early life, but in either case it was his absence that foiled him. While it was mysterious and exciting to a little girl—he could play the white knight with immunity—it became a sign of unreliability and inconstancy to a maturing adolescent. The seduction did not take hold and he was rejected as a father.

Meg rejected all men when she rejected Anthony, but she was extremely fortunate in discovering the spiritual life. It most probably saved her from a life of frustrated and possibly perverted sexuality.

Amy is thirty-six, overweight but pretty, quiet but determined, intimidatingly good at her job as a magazine editor, friendly with strangers, intimate with a few friends, strong-minded but sexually ambiguous. Her mother was diagnosed as having a fatal illness while carrying Amy and died six months after giving birth. Her father died ten years ago of a stroke; Amy admits to having no feelings about him at all.

For the first seven years of her life, Amy lived with a maternal uncle who spent most of his time on the road as a salesman, leaving the girl in the care of his wife, Eleanor. Aunt Eleanor was not happy with the arrangement, Amy felt, and left the girl mostly to her own devices, which meant alone. She recalls no friends before school, only intense solitude, playing on the floor with objects transformed into toys by her imagination, listening to the radio and imitating the songs she was hearing, learning to read early and devouring comic books, sitting quietly for hours at a time, fantasizing about the exploits of her favorite heroes.

Amy has but a few memories of her father during these years; he visited no more than once or twice a year, although he lived in the same town working as a clerk at the post office. He struck Amy as being both demanding and affectionate, always wanting to know everything his girl had been doing and thinking. His visits were not only rare but short and ended invariably with father forcibly tickling daughter, compelling her to laugh uncontrollably. Even today, Amy is angry at the memory of those tickling bouts, yet she is aware that at the time she had taken them as signs of his love for her.

At seven, her aunt and uncle's hospitality ran out and Amy was placed with another relative, widowed Aunt Ellen, with whom she was to spend the first three of her school years. This period is marked in Amy's memory as the time when she discovered that she was different from others; she was the only one in her class who did not have a mother and whose father bore no resemblance to other fathers. This discovery was a painfully embarrassing one and her classmates did not miss the opportunity of teasing her unmercifully.

Her father's visits did not increase in frequency during the years with Aunt Ellen and he became both more demanding and physically intimate. He inquired in great detail about Amy's progress in school and made sarcastic demands when her answers were unsatisfactory. His interrogations alternated with periods of fondling, which had now replaced tickling, and consisted of his asking for a "big hug," prolonged by his caressing his daughter's hair and back down to her buttocks. Amy was still taking these manifestations of presumably fatherly love as genuine expressions of affection, but as she talks about them today her hands tremble and there is a slight tic in her left eyelid.

Her anger at her father began to develop during these three years. She could not account for the rareness of his visits, nor for the way they were spent. If he was so interested in her school work, why did he not come more often and keep tabs on it? If he knew so much more than her teachers, as he claimed, then why did he not come and help her and teach her, instead of grilling her and teasing her ignorance with sarcasm? And, why did his embraces, which thrilled her so, make her so uncomfortable at the same time?

She would have liked to ask Aunt Ellen, but knew that she would be brushed off. Aunt Ellen was an artist, totally devoted to her paintings and their commercial disposition, and while she saw to it that Amy was properly dressed and fed and schooled, she would not extend her interests beyond her basic obligations. Questions were not encouraged—nothing was encouraged. Amy was embarrassed to ask her school-mates inside her house, for it was almost devoid of furniture, its walls hung thickly with paintings, its floors bare.

All of a sudden, at age ten, Aunt Ellen told Amy that she would be living with her father from now on. He had a good job now and a larger apartment, and wanted his little girl to be with him. Amy was angry and happy at the same time; angry because of his power to alter her life so drastically after so many years of neglect, and happy at the prospect of perhaps becoming a daughter like other daughters to a father like other fathers.

For the next seven years, Amy lived alone with her father in an atmosphere of constant unmitigated tension. Her expectations of change were frustrated almost immediately. He assigned her to a tiny room in an otherwise large if crumbling apartment, made out an exacting daily schedule that she was to follow scrupulously "or else," and every evening at eight she was to report to him on the events of her day. He gave her a meager allowance and expected her to provide for her lunch, shop for their dinner after school, cook it, and have it ready when he came home at six.

The routine was set on Amy's first day and continued for seven years. School was the redeeming factor during this period, for it allowed Amy to be herself to some extent, to exercise her intellect, to show off, to be praised, to form friendships, to learn about boys and sex, albeit secondhand, to be a young adolescent, and soon a young woman. She was a top student, and several teachers interested themselves in her future. One thought that she would make a good writer and encouraged her to compose short vignettes of what she thought and felt about things around her. This appealed to Amy and she spent the few minutes she could spare from her stringent routine in writing down her observations in shorthand, to save time.

By necessity, she also learned to cook well with simple ingredients; she regards this accomplishment as the sole positive result of her seven years with father. Today, when she can well afford to cook elegant meals for her friends, she still prides herself on serving lusty peasant meals that cost very little.

Their dinners, followed by the eight o'clock interrogatory session, lay "like a black cloud" over Amy's teen years. He never said a good word about the meals, although he invariably finished them, and usually sat through dinner in bleak silence, followed by an hour or so with the local tabloid, accompanied by excessive noise emanating from an unwatched television set. Then came the dreaded eight o'clock ritual. Amy had to sit next to him on the frayed sofa and recite the events of her day in chronological order, to be frequently interrupted by searching, sarcastic questions, such as, "And why, pray thee, did our precious Amy get a mere B — on her math quiz?" A shrug of the shoulders did not suffice for an answer, a precise explanation had to be given. All his questions were critical in the extreme, never indicating approval or encouragement, and Amy would feel pure, elemental hatred during these tortuous sessions. She developed migraine at eleven which persisted until she left for college seven years later.

Every Saturday night he left the house in the late evening and came back with a woman after Amy was presumably asleep, after midnight. It invariably woke her up and she would bury her head in pillows to drown out the sounds of their bawdy fornication; she had fantasies of killing him during these Saturday night bouts, always with a knife in his stomach. Other nights, she heard him masturbate, which disgusted her so much that she went to the bathroom and stayed there for a long time.

But worst of all were the evenings when he required her ministrations. He would pretend to be depressed or ill or having an ache in the back, and ask Amy to make him feel better. Sometimes, she would have to sit in his lap, held close by him, gently rocking side to side. Until she was about fifteen, Amy was able to enjoy this particular form of endearment, but not after that. His other requests sickened her from the beginning. His prescription for relieving depression called for his lying down on the sofa and placing his head in Amy's lap; he would then ask her to caress his

face with both hands, particularly his forehead and eyebrows, and then guide her hands down his chest and sides,
ending at the navel and hips. He never went beyond these
points, but when Amy was old enough to know, she could
clearly see him concealing his erection by crossing his legs.
She averted her eyes and thought of the knife in his stomach.

Once or twice a month, he feigned illness and called Amy
to his room, no matter what the hour. He would most often
claim to have a chill—his soul was chilled, he would say—
and ask Amy to warm him "back to life." She was compelled to lie down next to him in the bed, always wearing her
nightgown, and press against him—her front to his back or
her back to his front, never face to face. She would have to
stay for ten, fifteen minutes, suffer his concealed erections,
and then be allowed to return to her bed where she would
bite her nails till they bled.

Amy had nothing to fall back on but her migraine, which
protected her from reality. She could not discuss it with anyone, but she often described her feelings and perceptions in
her secret shorthand notebooks, which she has held on to
and still retains in a safety deposit box. Her will contains
provisions for their destruction.

Amy had great difficulty in getting away from her father
when it was time to go to college. Had it not been for a
scholarship that provided tuition, books, room, and board,
she might not have made it at all. He used threats of physical
restraint, pleaded poverty that could be relieved only with
the help of Amy's future earnings, even hinted at suicide.
But Amy's determination, fed by seven years of disgust, hu-
miliations, and hatred, could not be opposed and she entered
college far away from home. She saw her father only once
more in her life.

To her astonishment, Amy found in a matter of months
that her hatred for her father dissolved with distance. She
developed a pragmatic attitude—she *willed* to feel neither
love nor hate. She *willed* not to have guilt feelings when
time came for her father to die, and feels that she succeeded
completely in that respect. Having been out of touch with
him for some eight years, she got news of his fatal illness

and traveled a long distance to see him for the last time, more out of personal curiosity than sympathy. She found him in a terminal state, virtually paralyzed by a stroke, barely able to signal that he recognized his daughter with a hint of a smile, an almost imperceptible raising of a hand. She said nothing.

Amy states that she has not thought about her father for years prior to our conversations, although she is perfectly aware of the devastating influence he has exerted on her personal life. She first discovered this in her first year of college, her first year of being away from him, when she started dating. Going out with boys was totally out of the question while she was living with him; the impossible schedules he had established left not a single unaccounted-for minute, and it was otherwise made clear that dating was something for the future.

She looked forward eagerly to finding out about men and it did not take her long. She began with a modicum of suspicion and succeeded in staying at that level for some years. It was not until she was thirty that she knew that she would be angry at men for as long as she lived. She was and is able to enjoy sexual activity but incapable of forming personal bonds, and even her sexuality rests on the core of her anger, inasmuch as her enjoyment and anger are simultaneous and intermingled, just as she had been thrilled and confused at the same time by her father's early fondlings.

Amy does not think that she will marry, but believes in the possibility of successive two- to three-year liaisons, and that is all she is hoping for.

Amy's father—she never mentioned his name in our talks—has little in common either with Geoffrey or Anthony. His seductiveness was much cruder and more direct—it had an incestuous edge. Also, unlike the former, he appears to have been markedly neurotic, perhaps even schizoid. His absence from Amy's early life lacked the glamorous qualities of Anthony's, and when he was present he often spoiled the excitement by his nagging, obnoxious ways. Sarah and Meg never had to cope with physical manifestations of seductiveness, which was the bane of Amy's existence until she left for college, nor did their fathers exhibit the controlling, repressive aspects of Amy's father.

Amy's sexuality was affected in a way that lies somewhere between Sarah's and Meg's. She is neither promiscuous nor manipulative like the former, and she is not chaste like the latter. The same strength that enabled her to will her father out of her mind is making it possible for her to lead a relatively adequate sex life. Also, she is embarked on an apparently successful career, which has eluded both Sarah and Meg.

It is probably fortunate that Amy's life with father had a delayed beginning; had she been subjected to his behavior from infancy, without the cushioning presence of her mother, her present situation would undoubtedly be more troubled.

Jennifer is a twenty-six-year-old suburban housewife with two children under three. She married a man fifteen years older than she is four years ago, and their marriage has been an embattled one from the beginning. She is a nice-looking, nervous person, with much natural charm, but one has the feeling that she keeps looking over her shoulder for fear of pursuers.

She grew up in a suburb very much like the one she is living in now, the only child of working parents. Her father wanted to be a botanist, but there was no money and he ended up in the construction business, not very successfully. Her mother started a mail order business in their basement, and it grew into a very substantial enterprise, accounting for two thirds of the family's income. Mother was always Jennifer's friend, even though running the business was her first priority. Still, Jennifer felt free to run downstairs any time to visit mother, to ask her a question, to complain about the housekeeper, and was never made to feel that she was intruding.

Father was perceived as a "Sunday father," and his absence bothered Jennifer as far back as she could remember. When he was around, father was a yeller and a hitter. He wanted his girl to be perfect, and when she was not, he spanked her; still, she wanted him around more than he was, and in the hope of attaining her goal, she was a sweet child who always tried to do what was expected of her. She can remember as far back as three or four, and even then she made up excuses for her father's behavior. She imagined that he was very important in the world and every time he went home to his family, something dreadful happened which he had to fix when he returned on Monday. All her life she has been trying to understand father and she still does. Also, she has had a headache every Sunday since she was six or younger.

After lunch on Sundays her parents retired to their bedroom, which made little Jennifer very nervous. She could not imagine why both of them had to leave her alone for so long. They stopped this habit when she was in the second grade, and it relieved her immensely, although more time with father meant more spankings. She could always run to mother for solace and be sure that she would get it, yet she wondered why father was not hitting mother as well. Did that mean that he loved Jennifer more?

When she started school, she discovered that spanking was not regarded as desirable by her schoolmates and she was afraid to tell them that she did not mind, that she thought it was a normal part of what took place between fathers and children. In time, though, her resentment grew, and when in fourth grade the class was asked to write a composition on the subject of why they respected their fathers, Jennifer was unable to turn in more than a few sentences.

At the same time, she discovered that father was a drinker. She had noticed earlier that he smelled different from other people, but thought little of it. Now that she knew why, she was mortified and ashamed and took to holding her breath when she was near father. Meanwhile, the beatings continued into her teens, but she no longer regarded them as expressions of love and grew to abhor his touching her in any form.

She was also to find out, mainly from her mother's veiled remarks, that he bitterly resented the fact that the mother was the family's chief provider, and Jennifer was smart enough to figure out that in effect she was taking the brunt of her father's anger, which was aimed at her mother. It also became clear that her mother had always known this and felt terribly guilty about it; Jennifer learned the meaning of guilt from her.

She became a rebellious teenager; she disagreed with father about everything, but mother remained sympathetic, perhaps because she had no choice. She took extreme left political views, which infuriated her ultraconservative father, but her first serious boyfriend turned out to be just like him—unreasonable and punishing. In sharp contrast, his successor was sweet and understanding; when he tried to go too far, Jennifer would hit him in the face, not gently at all, which would spur him on even more. Eventually, she had her first sex at sixteen, vigorously and violently, with an older man. She would pound and claw his back whenever his ardor faded, and he would sometimes slap her around out of sheer frustration. Until her marriage, her sex life followed the same pattern: violent, stormy affairs alternating with quiet, friendly relationships with no sex. In the former, the men were tall and older, in the latter they were of her age, any size.

When Jennifer was asked whether she did not think that her life was too much in accordance with her perception of her father—even to the point of being suspiciously predictable—she replied that the thought had often occurred to her. She has long accepted the premise that an affair with a father figure would be followed by one with a mother figure—the latter atoning for the former. Then she revealed what she had been withholding.

When Jennifer was eighteen or nineteen, her somewhat inebriated father confided in her that he had not had sex with his wife for twelve years, and when they had had it, it was not good. Nor had he had any extramarital sex all those years; he was a bitter man, he said, bitter and frustrated and angry. His wife humiliated him with her success in business, and he was certain that she had lovers as well, although lacked proof. Jennifer was the only bright light in his life.

Soon after this confession, which left Jennifer shaky and guilty about her mother, she got pregnant by an older man; she had an abortion and did not tell anyone, but the experience really awakened her to the gravity of her situation. She felt that her father had seduced and deceived her all along, and at the same time she had misunderstood him completely, allowing him to set the pattern of her relationships with men. The spankings, which she took at first to be expressions of love for her, were in fact expressions of anger for her mother, his expectations of perfection from her were in fact directed at himself and therefore doomed to remain unfulfilled. It was like a catharsis, Jennifer says, worth ten years of psychoanalysis.

Not long after that, not having made any attempt at any sort of a career, Jennifer married her present husband, who struck her as a perfect combination of her parents. He has a penchant for occasional sadomasochistic sex, which is not frequent enough to be disturbing to Jennifer, and the rest of the time he is a devoted husband and father. Nevertheless, she is very fearful at times, fearful of frustration and misunderstandings, and blames her father for it "ninety-two percent." She sometimes thinks that her feelings for her husband are not genuine, that they are playing out a *folie à deux,* that love is beyond her capabilities. She plans to get some sort of help as soon as she has a chance.

Jennifer's father, Jerry, is a tall, good-looking man in his early fifties. He does not say much, except when in convivial company with convivial spirits on hand. He still spends much of his time away from home, living near construction sites he is associated with. It is clear that he does not like women. His conversation is laced with remarks such as, "Just like a woman," or "Only a woman would think of that." He is quick to bring his wife into conversations, referring to her as "the wife"; on the surface, he seems to be proud of the fact that she makes more money than he does, but hostile allusions are not far behind. "She didn't have to go through what I went through," he would say, or, "She can't take it but she can dish it out." He seems just as proud of his daughter at first blush; he is quick to brag about his son-in-law, the broker, but later he would say that he was perhaps a bit too old for her. "What is she going to do when he can't get it up anymore?" he would ponder.

By his account, he had a tough childhood and youth. He grew up on a farm where the land was poor and every blade of grass had to be extricated by hard labor. His mother died when he was not yet six, and the house was run by a maiden aunt and his two older sisters. He was helping his father in the fields as soon as he was able to lift a hoe, and his task-master was a stern one. His father would show him how to do a chore just once, and he was expected to know how to do it from then on. Failure was punished by quick and hard slaps; "his backhand was every bit as good as his fore-hand," Jerry says proudly.

He worked from dawn to dusk and was kept out of school at every opportunity to help out in the fields. He was a year late in finishing elementary school, and entered high school two years late. He speaks of missed school with regret; early on, he developed an interest in plants and flowers and yearned to learn more about them, but there was no time. He pleaded with his father to get him some books on botany as soon as he learned what the word meant, but it was all in vain. He was a hard man, an unreasonable man. Even when a high school teacher, who was impressed with Jerry's self-acquired knowledge of flowers and plants, tried to persuade his father to encourage the boy's interest, he remained unconvinced. He needed the boy in the fields—and that was that.

He got to be a very good farmer, he says, but this was never acknowledged by his father. Everything that went right had been expected to go right and required no praise or even notice; only things that went wrong were recognized because they went contrary to expectations—therefore, they had to be someone's fault, and that someone had to be punished for them. Life was clear and simple to Jerry's father. There was work; it had to be done well; there was nothing more to it.

His older sisters were of great comfort to Jerry. They spoiled him behind their father's back with goodies they had cooked and baked for him, and on Sundays when father went to visit his few friends they had a good time running free in the house and the barn. They went to bed early on Sundays, because father would invariably come home drunk and it was best to stay out of his way. Jerry learned that much could be expected of women, but they could not defend him against his father's power.

When the Korean War came, Jerry managed to enlist secretly and left without saying good-bye to anyone. He was afraid to trust his sisters or aunt; he thought they might betray him just to keep him home. He had a tough war and saw a lot of combat, but came through all right. He learned to value camaraderie between men, and having "good drinking buddies" became important to him then and now. His first sexual experiences with Korean prostitutes pleased him immensely; at last he found out what women were all about.

When he came home he wrote his father and sisters. The only answers came from his sisters, both of them married to farmers within fifty miles of home. They said father had died a few months after he left; he got pneumonia after a severe winter and died in a matter of days. Jerry regrets that he did not get to know his father "like a man should," and speaks of him with respect.

He married a woman admittedly smarter than himself, but was gravely disappointed that she could not duplicate the accomplishments of Korean prostitutes. He tried local prostitutes, but they were not satisfactory either, and a few years after his daughter was born, he gave up sex altogether. Drinking with good friends seemed a much more rewarding way of spending one's time.

He still regrets that he missed out on botany and is betrayed by his daughter's failure to turn into something. He thinks she should have had a career instead of marrying some "old goat." He tried to encourage her when she was young, even tried "to beat some sense into her," but without success. He is bitter about that and, he says confidentially, he really has no use for women.

On the face of it, it seems that Jennifer's father would be more comfortable if he had been placed in the chapter on tyrannical, demanding fathers. He certainly had tyrannical and demanding qualities, but Jennifer definitely classified him as seductive and assigns all blame to him for her sexual peculiarities.

Sunday fathers are invariably seductive to their daughters, because their absence can so easily be explained by endowing them with romantic or mysterious characteristics. In Jennifer's case, she imagined him to be a man of great importance in the world, which suffered from his Sunday absences. Consequently, beatings could be regarded in a sense as an atonement for keeping him from his more important tasks.

Psychoanalysts might reject Jennifer's "catharsis," which revealed to her that by beating her her father was expressing anger toward her mother, and suggest instead that the beatings were applied to ward off his incestuous desires. His sexual confession to her, which could be construed as a proposition, reinforces such an interpretation.

Others might hold the view that beatings were associated in Jerry's mind with imperfect execution of orders, and he was merely adopting his father's methods when he beat his daughter. Besides, he may have been expressing his frustrations at failing to become a botanist and at being financially inferior to his wife. Whichever the case, the beatings had a sexual connotation for Jennifer, and her most successful sexual experiences were with father figures. She does not even seem to notice that she foiled his expectations of her, as he was foiled in his own by his father.

tyrannical, demanding

Peter is a musician. He is the concertmaster of a major symphony orchestra, and has been for some fifteen years. He also teaches at a distinguished conservatory, and a number of his students are in the process of building international reputations on the concert stage. He is in his early sixties, a commanding figure with bushy eyebrows, an intimidatingly shining dome of a head, expressive deep-set eyes, and bony limbs. When he plays the violin, he assumes an austere expression of face, a rigid posture of body, as if his whole being were absolutely concentrated in the next note to be played.

Peter grew up in Western Europe, the son of a famous pianist who was almost equally famous for his refusal to perform away from his native city. He had a travel phobia and refused even to enter automobiles and trains, not to say planes. He gave four concerts annually and admirers came from all over Europe to hear him play. In the 1930s, he made several series of studio recordings that are considered collector's items today.

His only son gave evidence of musical talent at a very early age and was encouraged, though not pushed, to explore and expand it. He learned the basic rudiments of piano playing from his father and was then passed on to a professional teacher, studying not only the instrument itself, but also music theory and history. By age seven, Peter was an accomplished pianist, deeply interested in composing—a serious little boy, obedient to his parents, and seemingly devoting himself to the service of classical music. He was a good student, but more out of a sense of duty than interest in subjects other than music.

Peter was deeply devoted to his father and the father strongly attached to the boy. He often sat in on his music lessons, but never interfered; each night, he came to Peter's room after bedtime and read him a story. As the boy grew older, the stories became more literary, progressing as far as Dickens, Balzac, and Dumas; he was reading from volume four of a ten-volume edition of Romain Rolland's *Jean-Christophe* when he died suddenly of a heart attack, sitting in a chair next to Peter's bed. He was still in his forties and the boy was thirteen.

Fifty years later, Peter still speaks about his father with unmistakable affection and respect. He recalls the extraordinarily long walks his father used to take him on, sometimes lasting two to three hours; they talked mostly about music, ranging over such topics as the mysteries of harmony and counterpoint, as well as amusing anecdotes about Brahms or Dohnányi or Bruno Walter. The boy would be exhausted but exhilarated at the end of these walks because his father generally played the piano for him after they got home.

He stopped playing the piano when his father died and has not touched one since. His love of music was compellingly strong, though, and he was soon studying the violin with the encouragement of his mother, who played the instrument herself. Peter has little else to say about his mother; she seemed not to have played an important role in his life. She remained home after Peter came to America. She died during World War II.

fathers

When Peter was asked if he had any memories of his father that were unrelated to music or to their nightly literary excursions, he said there were hardly any. There were no physical demonstrations of love and affection and he could not recall other topics of conversation. Then he suddenly remembered that during one of their long walks they stopped to pee in the snow. The arc of the father's stream ended much farther away than the boy's, which made him both envious and proud. But then the father said, "Soon you will be able to pee much farther than I," and the boy was no longer envious, only proud.

By the time Peter graduated from high school, Hitler was looming large in Europe, and it was decided that he should continue his musical studies in America. He was able to obtain a scholarship at an excellent conservatory and was dispatched in care of a distant but interested relative who lived in the same city. He arrived at the age of nineteen, saturated with music and the memory of his father, but lacking other concerns or ties to people. He was eager to become a first-rate violinist and a respected musician, one his father could be proud of.

It was not long before Peter learned that his aspirations were not to be fully realized. After his first year at the conservatory it was made clear to him by his principal violin teacher that it would be prudent of him to set his sights lower; he was going to be an excellent violinist, but not a first-rate soloist with a concert career. Similarly, his grasp of the principles of composition was highly praised, but it was held unlikely that he could develop into an original composer.

Peter was dejected to the point of contemplating giving up music altogether. But he looked around in the world and found no substitute; he tried working at various jobs in commerce and banking but found them arid, inconsequential. After a year of uncertainty and sadness, he decided to become a superb teacher of the violin and to take his talent as a performer no further than it could rationally go. He was aided in his decision by a young immigrant woman he had met at the conservatory who came from within a hundred miles of his hometown and was a student of the flute. She told Peter that their children would all become brilliant musicians and that his pupils would spread praise of their wonderful teacher all around the world.

Sheila and Peter got married when they were both in their mid-twenties, soon after they both landed jobs in the same orchestra—an accomplishment made easier by the wartime draft, from which Peter, as a foreign citizen, was exempt. Their firstborn, Robert, was born a year later, followed at two-year intervals by Beatrice and Alfred. Sheila and Peter, who had come together on the strength of their mutual love of music and cared for little else, now had to expand their vistas and broaden their horizons to make room for three infinitely moldable yet unpredictable children. According to Peter, they both realized what they were facing at the time and proceeded to deal with it methodically and reasonably.

Robert is now thirty-seven. He is the sole American licensee of a foreign piano manufacturer and is doing extremely well financially. He entered the piano business when he was twenty-five, after he gave up music for good. He is on cool terms with his parents, especially his mother, and sees them only a few times a year. He is happily married, has two children of no discernible musical talents, and has no plans for providing them with instruction in music.

Robert was not eager to talk about his childhood and youth. He winced and fidgeted a lot when he was finally persuaded to collect his memories, and his right foot tapped rhythmically as if keeping time to an inaudible tune. He is tall and skinny, outwardly nervous but inwardly calm. He has chosen his course in life after tremendous turmoil and anguish and is seemingly content with his choice.

By his account, Robert's childhood was a nightmare. His very first memory is that of being placed on a piano bench by his mother, propped between pillows and sitting on cushions, for he was too tiny to reach the keyboard or even to sit up straight by himself. He did not take to music naturally and had to be cajoled and later ordered to practice regularly. He remembers hardly anything about his first five years other than facing the keyboard, practicing unending scales, and hearing first his mother's whiny voice and later his father's sonorous instructions. It had been made quite clear to him as soon as he could understand words that he descended from a musically prominent family and was expected to continue the tradition. It took hard, almost constant, practice, he was told, but there was nothing else worth doing and his rewards would be enormously gratifying.

After the age of five, he was placed entirely under his father's guidance. He was not allowed to go anywhere after school, neither to play with or visit friends nor to participate in extracurricular activities. He had to come straight home and practice for four hours before dinner; on weekends he had to practice six hours a day, on vacations from four to six. His father sat next to him virtually all the time—instructing, correcting, humming, fussing. No one at home paid any attention to his school work and grades, and there was little talk of any subject but music.

Robert's life was filled with dreading the next time he had to sit down at the piano; his school hours, even his sleep, were permeated with fear. He would dream of gigantic pianos rolling toward him, and wake up with a start or an outcry just before they crushed him to death. He cannot recall a single moment when he enjoyed playing or practicing; his only pleasure was basketball during intermissions at school. His friendships were restricted to school hours, and there were few anyway. His schoolmates taunted him a great deal for having to rush home from school and called him "sissy" and "queer" for playing the piano.

He was too afraid of his father to ask him to let him give up music. He listened all too often to Peter's tales of admiration about his own father, and how his death had such a paralyzing effect on him that he could not touch the piano again. It was up to Robert to take on and expand his grandfather's career and to build the family's already famous surname into a legend. The father's exhortations were frequently supplemented by his mother's, with the added burden of his being told by her that Peter himself was a great musician who had chosen teaching over a concert career and looked to his son to attain fame on the concert stage.

By the time Robert was twelve or so, it was becoming increasingly evident that he was not touched by genius. His talent was decidedly minor, but his father would not give up, citing great musicians of the past who were late bloomers. At that time, he was also occupied with the musical education of Beatrice and Alfred, and Robert was passed on to a teacher at the conservatory where his father was working. His progress did not accelerate, and it was only as a favor to Peter that he was kept on as a pupil.

Robert was not allowed to go to high school, in a desperate attempt to lure the genius that must have been concealed deep within him out of its lair. He was tutored privately and superficially, with twelve hours of each day, six days a week, devoted to music. He struggled ferociously and at the same time hopelessly, knowing that the day was near when everyone would know that he had let his family down; there was not going to be a glorious concert career, not even an ordinary one. He could see the same thing happening to his sister, whose combat with the cello was taking place in a small room at the other end of the house. They exchanged anguished glances at the dinner table, but they did not really get to know each other until years later.

At fifteen, Robert's health broke down. Pneumonia, asthma, and a rheumatic heart condition struck in rapid succession, and he had to spend nearly a year in and out of bed at home and at hospitals. Playing the piano was now out of the question, as were all physical exertions. Deep inside, Robert felt blissful relief concealed by layers of guilt at having failed his father and grandfather and having disappointed his mother. All he had to do was look at his parents' faces to confirm his guilt: His father was aging visibly, his mother shrinking like a drying sponge. They said nothing to him and they did not have to. They appeared to be unconcerned about his health; they faded away from him and retreated into their own miseries.

Robert was eighteen by the time he could return to playing the piano for any length of time, and by that time his father had given up hope for an important career for him. Still, he was sent back to the conservatory to study theory and composition, for if he was not to become a serious composer, he could at least develop into an important teacher. He continued to live in daily anguish, relieved only by not having to practice the piano and thereby gaining a few hours of free time, most of which was spent in schoolyards, playing basketball. He hated his music studies and never listened to music when he did not have to, but, of course, he did have to so long as he lived at home where even the bathrooms were equipped with pairs of speakers.

He hardly ever spoke to his parents, and their concern for him, which was always confined to music, was now further restricted to perfunctory inquiries about his composition class. He got to know his sister, Beatrice, and brother, Alfred, a little better, although they had little time to talk to him about their lives. Beatrice seemed to like playing the cello more than she used to, but Alfred had rebelled successfully against music and was developing into a brilliant mathematician. He was hardly ever home, and when he was, his nose was buried in books and papers. Peter and Sheila walked about the house like tragic figures, defeated by destiny.

At twenty-one, Robert asked his father to be allowed to get his own apartment; he was going to continue his studies and support himself with a job as a salesman of musical instruments. He expected to be denied, but his father seemed almost relieved to give his permission for the move, provided Robert did not abandon his music studies. Robert found a place of his own very quickly, and his furnishings did not include any musical instrument, stereo equipment, or sheet music.

He was beginning to get acquainted with other aspects of life and discovered that he liked women, Proust, the theater, and, more than ever, basketball. He bought a season's ticket to the local professional team's home games and attended them religiously. He slept with a woman for the first time when he was twenty-two and his repressed sexuality came into full bloom. He thinks of himself as having been born at twenty-one and therefore enjoying life with greater intensity than other people do.

Step by step, Robert was withdrawing from his music studies. He attended classes less and less, failed to do his assignments, and was inattentive; he would have flunked out, no doubt, had it not been for the presence of his father on the faculty. To avoid a confrontation, he stopped going to classes altogether without saying anything to the school or to his father, and his departure was politically ignored by both. No one said anything, and his life in music was over just as his life in the business of music began.

He had done very well as a salesman of musical instruments, and now he began to specialize in pianos, which led him to his present position. He married at thirty, having carefully chosen a woman who had no pronounced interest in music while having the capacity to enjoy it. There is no piano in their house, and if the children should prove to have musical talent, it would have to manifest itself without parental pressure or even encouragement.

Robert appears to be exceedingly bitter about the first twenty-one years of his life and blames his father as well as his mother for his past miseries. He has tried to understand Peter in the light of his heritage and his self-assumed role of propagating his father's interrupted career, but he cannot forgive him. He would feel differently, he thinks, if Peter's father had charged him with the obligation of perpetuating music as the family's bloodstream; his tyranny could then be understood at least. But having assigned himself a role that could be played out only at the cost of dominating and manipulating his children's lives, Peter has placed himself beyond the boundaries of forgiveness. This is especially so for Robert, because he is convinced that only his lack of musical talent saved him from a lifetime of misery, as well as enabled him to make a contented life for himself.

When Robert is asked if he finds any irony in the fact that the grandson of a great pianist and the son of a great music teacher has chosen the career of selling pianos, he admits that he does. On the one hand, he is continuing the tradition of music as the "family business," in a manner that could only be regarded as humiliating by his father, thereby repaying him for twenty-one years of anguish; yet on the other hand, he has chosen his career of his own free will. He did not choose to sell bonds, he did not choose to sell real estate, he chose to sell pianos—symbols of the family tradition. "A psychoanalyst could do a lot with that," he said with a smile.

Beatrice is thirty-five and internationally known as a concert cellist. She travels thirty weeks each year on tours around the world, and teaches two or three promising cellists while she is home. She makes it a rule to spend at least two weeks each year with her parents at their summer vacation house.

Her early memories are not unlike Robert's. She remembers her mother as constantly playing the flute for her, or humming melodies that Beatice had to imitate, or singing songs that she had to learn. Often, she and Peter played violin and flute duos for her and she had to hum the pieces for them afterward. If she could not, they would play it again and again, until she got it right. As soon as she was physically able to handle a cello, her lessons began. She did not like them and played only to please her parents, especially her father; he seemed so eager for her to play well. Also, she seemed to have a knack for the instrument and did not have to practice for hours to learn a new piece.

As was the case with Robert, her schooling was ignored by her parents. They did not care what grades she brought home so long as she came straight home from school. She resented this because she liked school, did well, and had good friends; by the time she was seven or eight, she was keenly hostile to her mother, although she kept it to herself. At the same time, she could not help but love her father—he looked so wounded when she made a mistake in her playing, so proud when she played well. She was determined to do well by him always.

All this time, her playing was purely mechanical and her feelings toward the cello no more than neutral. She did not hate it and she did not look forward to practicing and playing; she did resent that she had to spend so much time on it when she could have been having fun with her friends. She dismissed her resentment by thinking of daddy.

She could handle a full-size cello by the time she was ten, and her serious training at the conservatory began. For the first time, she was told that her talent for her instrument was exceptional, a fact unrecognized by her parents, neither of whom was expert enough about cello playing. They knew enough to realize that she was good, but not enough to see how good. This changed everything for Beatrice. Suddenly—she claims it happened in a flash—she discovered that all these years she had been playing *music,* not the cello. It was a revelation, and from then on her life was given over to music. She practiced and studied with a passion, no longer resentful about not having fun, no longer interested in school. Her parents were ecstatic, and when she won first prize at an international competition when she was seventeen, her father embraced her for the first time in her life.

Beatrice pursued her concert career wholeheartedly and attained her present prominence by her late twenties. She says she is very happy and fully satisfied with her life and that she does not need men. She claims never to have had any sexual stirrings or fantasies, and certainly no experience with men or women. She plans to continue her life as it is now, wholly devoted to music. She loves her parents, especially her father, although she believes they went about her early musical training in the wrong way: They were too forceful and emphasized the technical mastery of the instrument over the meaning of the music. She also believes that they were quite wrong to push Robert and Alfred the way they did, especially after they had seen that the boys lacked talent, but she readily forgives them by virtue of her father's history and her mother's total devotion to him and to music, to the exclusion of all else.

Alfred is the youngest in the family and that alone accounts for his exemption from the tyranny of music. By the time he became four and ready for his parents' ministrations, Robert was already close to revealing his lack of talent and desire, and Beatrice too undeveloped musically to show clear promise. Peter and Sheila were at a stage where it seemed that the dreams they had forged for their children might dissolve into disillusionment and they were close to despair. As a result, they approached Alfred's musical education more cautiously than they had Robert's and Beatrice's.

They decided that Alfred, too, should take on the piano, for Robert's failure was already apparent, and this was their last chance, or so they thought at the time, to continue the family's musical tradition in the professional sense. Alfred recalls his early struggles with the piano with an air of vagueness, which is his dominant characteristic. He does not remember his mother hovering about him, but clearly recollects his father's stern demands for a correctly played scale.

Like Robert and Beatrice, Alfred did not develop a fondness for his instrument. He felt badgered and oppressed earlier than the other children had, because, as he says, his personality was made of sterner stuff than theirs. He had a clear sense of not wanting to do as he was instructed by the time he entered elementary school, where his father's demands were multiplied by those of the school, arousing Alfred's innate need for personal freedom. He rebelled first in school, which was easier, by persistently violating rules of conduct and refusing to learn what he did not want to know.

When news of his behavior reached home, the reaction was mild. His father told him that the law required that Alfred attend school, and that being the case he should at least obey the rules and not let the demands of school interfere with his musical education. His father's reaction led Alfred to realize that if he was to make a stand in his own behalf, it would have to be made at home; school was not the real scene of the struggle, home was. And so, his next step was to refuse to play the piano or even sit by it.

His first refusal brought on an outburst of rage from his father. He turned quite pale, Alfred recalls, then seized the boy, shook him by the shoulders, and forcibly put him down on the piano bench, facing the keyboard, all the while shouting something about duty and responsibility and the sanctity of music. Alfred was frightened at first, but did not give in. He shielded his head with his arms in anticipation of the blows he was sure to receive, and sat there without saying a word or moving. The blows did not come, but his father continued to shout at him, evoking the legend of the boy's grandfather, his own obedience to the family tradition, Robert's and Beatrice's valiant efforts to master their instruments, Sheila's love of music and her expectations of brilliance from her children, and even lying to Alfred by stating that he was the most talented of them all.

Frightened as he was, Alfred felt great pity for his father, but also sensed that he was lying and desperate. He was determined not to give in, and he claims that even then he had known that not only did he lack the desire to play the piano, he also realized that he would be adding to his father's anguish if he continued to play and showed no talent. These two factors reinforced each other and combined into a double resolve not to give in. He remained mute through his father's harangue and showed no reaction when he said all he had to say. He was then told that he would be locked in his room with the piano for four hours each day, whether he practiced or not. There was a hint of some unnamed reward in case he chose to behave sensibly.

For four whole months, Alfred spent his afternoons locked in his room and never even looking at the piano. It was during this period that, out of desperate boredom, he began dabbling in mathematics. He had picked up a book of math problems and found to his amazement that he could solve them at will, without knowing what he was actually doing. This cheered him up immensely and he began to accumulate books on the subject, devouring them hungrily. Without a doubt, he had a natural talent for the subject; moreover, he actually found pleasure in it. He felt a great relief; he knew he was going to win the struggle with his father, he knew he was going to be freed of music.

He made his newly discovered talent known to his arithmetic teacher, and news of his wizardry soon swept the school and reached the ears of his parents. Alfred expected them not to pay attention, for mathematics could not compare with music in their estimation, and at first he was right. They did not display any interest, and Alfred's confinement continued for another month or more. Then, whether by the pressure of his teachers or as a result of further assessment of Alfred's talent, probably both, his parents relented and agreed to cooperate with the school in developing his potential in mathematics.

During the next several years, as Alfred was being confirmed as a legitimate math prodigy, his parents made an intellectual effort to admit mathematics into their scheme of values. His father decided that it had in fact a great deal in common with music in that both musical notation and the concept of time intervals and rhythm were mathematical in nature. In time, he grew quite enthused with his newly formed notions and one day announced that Bach's music was pure mathematics.

This process took place when Alfred was ten or eleven, and he recollects thinking to himself that his father had capitulated; he had forgiven Alfred and expected to be forgiven in turn. But forgiveness is not part of Alfred's nature, and he found his father's attempts to ingratiate himself pathetic. He kept aloof from his parents throughout his adolescence and still does. He sees them only on special occasions, such as a concert by Beatrice, Robert's wedding, an occasional Christmas.

Unlike Robert and Beatrice, Alfred is possessed of an intense sexuality—a subject he is eager to bring up at every opportunity. He has been sexually active since age thirteen when he spent money given to him by his father for school supplies on a prostitute. Ever since then, he has relieved the intellectual tension generated by his work in mathematics with sexual forays which became more and more varied. He admits that thoughts of his father play a part in his choice of sexual relief; he always wonders whether his father would enjoy or dislike what he is doing sexually. He rather thinks that Peter is quite satisfied with the missionary position and would be shocked by Alfred's appetite for variety. He proudly mentions his monthly visits to a talented dominatrix where he happily submits to various kinds of abuse, including oral castigation for which he prepares the text in advance. He also has brief but intense relationships with women of his age which are primarily sexual and in which he plays the dominant partner. He cannot imagine that he will ever marry, sees no reason why he should. Mathematics and sex fill his life quite satisfactorily.

His present view of his father is deliberately vague, as if he has not yet come to a conclusion. He definitely condemns him for using Robert as a "laboratory rat" and almost destroying him in the process. He feels that Beatrice, too, was used for the same purpose, except that this time "he got lucky." Her talent has saved both of them; her from a lifetime of misery, him from a lifetime of frustration and humiliation. As for himself, Alfred feels that he saved himself by his own sheer will, so markedly missing in Robert and Beatrice. He prefers not to have to despise or hate his father, but is not yet certain how he will feel in the future.

Peter talked freely about his children on several occasions, but each time he made it evident that he did not want his wife to be present. He arranged the timing and setting of our talks in such a way that Sheila could not be present, for which he apologized, even though it had been made clear to him that he alone was the subject of our talks. He said by way of introduction that he was pleased with the way his children have turned out, "on the whole." Robert was a successful businessman, Beatrice a world-class cellist, Alfred a brilliant mathematician. They chose careers in different segments of endeavor, and each one succeeded in his or her choice. When he was asked if he would have preferred to see all his children become musicians, he said no without hesitation. The way it turned out, the family tradition was being carried on by Beatrice, and he felt certain that Alfred's mathematical genius was the fountainhead of a new tradition to be followed by someone in the next generation. He believes that both music and mathematics are carried in the genes, and hopes to live long enough to see a successor to Beatrice and one to Alfred. He did not mention Robert's business as a possible source of family tradition, but he did seem genuinely pleased at his success in a line that was previously untested by earlier generations.

In striking contrast to Robert's account, Peter said that his first son took to the piano instinctively. He could barely crawl when he began gravitating toward the piano, and fell off the piano bench many times before he learned to sit up. As soon as he could reach the keyboard he started poking at the keys and spent much of his time doing it. In Peter's recollection, he and Sheila did not start systematic lessons until Robert was five, and the boy proved to be a quick study and fond of practicing several hours a day. They hoped that the boy would follow in his grandfather's footsteps and become a major concert artist, but he asserted that "such things cannot be forced," and all he and his wife were doing was to direct him toward the source of his talent and hope for the best.

He admitted that Robert's schooling was not taken very seriously because they took it for granted that Robert's career was going to be in music and they regarded school as a waste of time. "Musicians can always acquire other interests once they are established," he noted, and cited Arthur Rubenstein and Vladimir Horowitz as examples. He could not recall any instance when Robert objected to the schedule that was established for him.

He was beginning to get uncertain about Robert's future when the boy was about ten. Real talent makes itself known by that age, but Robert was showing no progress after age eight, and colleagues at the conservatory were politely unenthusiastic. This was a very difficult time for Peter and Sheila as they were totally unprepared to accept the likelihood that Robert was without sufficient talent for a concert career. When he was asked how he felt about Robert in other respects, he seemed startled. After a pause, he said that in the culture he and Sheila were brought up in the main consideration of parents was to have the eldest son follow in his father's footsteps. If he did, he "turned out well," if he did not, he "failed." The fulfillment of expectations was really the only thing that mattered; if the son was handsome or of pleasant temperament, that was a blessing; if he was sickly or of mean disposition, that was an obstacle that had to be overcome. "Feelings may be fashionable these days," he said, "but they are not important when one is bringing up a son with a definite purpose."

It was clear that Robert was perceived as a failed son, and that Peter was conveying Sheila's judgment as well. They still would not accept the apparent fact that Robert lacked musical talent, which is genetically transmitted, they believe. Peter is convinced that it was not the absence of talent that "turned Robert into what he is," but lack of discipline. He did not have the strength of character, the disciplined dedication, that distinguish true concert artists from piano players. Peter did not deny or regret that he was an extremely demanding father to Robert; what he regrets is his son's failure to respond to his demands.

Talking about Beatrice is much easier for Peter than talking about Robert. He regards her as the redeemer of the family tradition, yet finds it ironic that the role was assigned to a daughter while two sons chose different paths. When he was asked why he picked the cello as Beatrice's instrument instead of, say, the violin, which is physically much easier for a woman to master, he was evasive. He said that there had never been a serious cellist in the family and it was time to experiment and find out if there could be one, but it was evident from numerous other remarks that the choice of cello was a deliberate decision *not* to train a daughter for a piano career. Peter does not think highly of woman pianists and made a point of emphasizing that there has never been a woman pianist who belonged in the same class as Schnabel or Cortot or Horowitz. Clearly, he did not want to risk another failure, especially with Alfred just two years behind Beatrice.

Nevertheless, he felt a great relief when Beatrice showed signs of genuine talent. It justified his belief in the genetic inheritance of musical ability and maintained his conviction that Robert lacked discipline, not talent. Besides, the family name would be carried on on the concert stage, and he extracted a promise from Beatrice that her future children would retain the family name as their middle name—a fact not mentioned by unmarried Beatrice. He professed great pride in his daughter, but it was also evident that her success had taken him by surprise.

If astonished pride is the undertone of Peter's feelings toward Beatrice and that of discreet disappointment toward Robert, his professed pleasure at Alfred's successes seems propped up by a layer of bitterness. He takes Alfred's resistance to music personally, as if the boy rejected him by using music for an excuse. At the same time, he recognizes that the "strength of character and discipline" so sadly lacking in Robert is abundantly evident in Alfred's personality, and only the bitter tinge of his voice betrays his disappointment that this admirable trait was not devoted to the service of music. He appears to be in awe of Alfred's individuality, more so than he is of Beatrice's talent. He said nothing about his present frequency of contacts with either Robert or Beatrice, but said twice that he wished that he and Alfred were in closer touch.

As a boy, Peter idealized his father and was shattered when he lost him. So strong was his grief that he stopped playing the instrument he was trained for and never touched it again. A few years later, he suffered another traumatic loss when it became clear that his talent for the violin was not marked enough for a concert career. At that low point in his life, he met and married a kindred soul with whose help he was able to focus such talent as he had onto a teaching career.

When their three children came, Peter and Sheila made a decision that was to underlie the destinies of all three. The decision to propagate the tradition set by the interrupted career of Peter's father—a task he was not charged with— could only be carried out in the children's lives and was, therefore, irresponsible. It was determined from the day of their births that they would be manipulated and tyrannized, even if they were born with genius for music.

They were not born with genius, and the first two, Robert and Beatrice, were afflicted with a hellish childhood. Robert suffered longest, because, as the firstborn, he had special responsibilities which he failed to carry. He resolved the severe conflict between guilt and the needs of his own life by finding a niche at a lower rung of music, just as Renoir's son became a filmmaker and his grandson a cameraman. Beatrice was saved when she discovered music on her own, and Alfred when he discovered mathematics, although his innate strength of character might have saved him in any case.

Peter is not unduly troubled by the havoc he brought on his children's heads, even if his version of Robert's early years might indicate guilt, covered up by denial. Beatrice's success is a source of pride and self-justification for him, but he would clearly be happier if the source were Robert or Alfred. Peter is a man who learned nothing from his mistakes and would gladly do it all over again.

Ralph is a toolmaker in his sixties. He lives in the same small town in the Midwest he was born in and commutes to work in the large industrial city some fifty miles away. He is a small man whose waist has caught up with his broad shoulders and gives the impression of being physically very strong. His wife fades into the background of housekeeping; his behavior toward her and her own attitude make it clear that she truly believes that the woman's place is in the kitchen.

Ralph has always been a working man as his father was, yet he moved upward in the ranks. His father was an unskilled factory hand in the same plant in which Ralph is now a foreman with a skilled trade. He takes great pride in his position and credits his father with having instilled a powerful work ethic in his children—Ralph was the eldest of four. There was always enough to eat and decent clothes to wear, even though Ralph's mother was not allowed to work, because Ralph Senior always had a second job. Also, he went hunting every weekend and almost invariably bagged enough game for the family's meat supply. Ralph grew up on a diet of rabbit, possum, deer, wild duck, and the like; he did not taste beef or pork until he was in his mid-teens, and he has never yet tasted veal. All the children had to work after school as soon as they were able and had to contribute every cent they earned to the family budget. Ralph and his two brothers worked at pumping gas, in bowling alleys, in pizza parlors, in diners, while his sister, the youngest, did baby-sitting and later worked in luncheonettes as a waitress. With all of them working and mother doing all the cooking, cleaning, canning, and marketing, the family was a cohesive economic unit, self-supporting at the level of decent poverty.

Ralph has a gleam in his eyes when he talks about his youth; he recalls it as being very happy. He always enjoyed working and got a lot of satisfaction out of contributing to the family budget, as all the children were imbued early with the importance of making their own way by paying their own way—their father's favorite motto. He was close to his brothers and sister, all of whom still live within one hundred miles of their hometown; one brother is a master mechanic, the other a village police chief, and the sister, married to a civil servant, a mother of three.

Ralph Senior was extremely strict but not cruel or abusive. He did not have to be; one glance from him and they all jumped. There were no arguments between the parents either. All father had to do was ask for something and mother did it. He was not home much on account of his multiple jobs, but when he was, it counted for a lot. The children had to furnish a financial statement, accounting for every penny earned and spent each week, and from their father's comments they were able to derive the limits of what were acceptable and unacceptable ways of behavior. According to Ralph, none of the children ever deviated from the path laid out for them, none rebelled against their father's rules in adolescence or later.

As the sons grew older, they were allowed to accompany father on his hunting trips and each became a crack shot and a careful hunter; to Ralph, the opening of the deer hunting season is still the highlight of the year. On Saturday afternoons, when Ralph Senior was usually home, he was wont to put on his World War I uniform, shoulder his rifle, and drill the boys in the intricacies of marching and saluting in their small backyard. When the Korean War came, he urged the boys to enlist, even though Ralph and his brothers were all married by then, and Ralph's wife was three months pregnant. They enlisted unhesitatingly and served well; all came home with wounds and decorations.

As Ralph recalls it, there was very little conversation between his parents beyond discussions of household matters. His mother was totally compliant and seemed content, and when Ralph became engaged he was aware of the similarities between his fiancée and his mother. He still is and glad of it. He likes women to be that way. His father had warned him about "loose women," and he always heeded the advice, restricting his sexual activity to guilty masturbation until his wedding night. Ralph Senior told him before the wedding that women pretend they do not like sex but "want it" all the time in secret; he was advised "not to take any nonsense" from his wife and to "get his" whenever he fancied it. That advice, too, proved to be perfectly sound for Ralph Junior.

Ralph was in Korea when he got word that his wife gave birth to a baby girl—Christine, now thirty. It surprised him, because he sort of took it for granted that he would have many sons, but he was not displeased. A year after his return, his second child was born, another girl—Teresa, now twenty-seven. This time, Ralph was seriously disturbed; here he was, already in his thirties, with two daughters. By his own account, he then began "to pump" his wife at every opportunity, but nothing happened. It turned out that her tubes were blocked and further pregnancies were not possible.

Ralph was unhappy, confused, and his condition was further aggravated when his father died suddenly at work. He needed his father's advice badly, and felt shocked and abandoned by his unexpected death; he was also angry at his wife, blaming her for failing to give him sons. He got into the habit of stopping for a few beers after work, and went hunting and fishing with his buddies almost every weekend. It took him a couple of years to get over the fact that he was going to have two daughters for the rest of his life and that he was not going to have sons, ever. He persuaded himself that his father would have wanted him to "put his shoulder to the wheel and make the best of a bad job." He was going to do his best to bring up his daughters properly, and one day perhaps they were going to give him grandsons. It also helped him that his wife would be just the kind of mother girls needed in these troubled times.

Christine lives in a large city, and at the tender age of thirty she is the only female vice-president at a multinational corporation. She considers herself a workaholic, has few friends, practices hit-and-run sex during business trips and vacations, and plans to marry when she is past forty. She will not have children, nor marry a divorced man who has any of his own. She is not conventionally good-looking, but her vigor and forceful intellect combine with her sharp sense of humor to make her more than ordinarily attractive.

Christine refused to answer questions about her father directly and chose to record her memories and feelings on a tape cassette, unaided by questions, rather impressionistically. She claims she seldom thinks about her parents, calls them at Christmas and on their birthdays, and has not seen them in three years.

Her first memory of her father is clear: He stands by her playpen and shouts at her. She does not know why. Later, she learns that he shouts at her for any reason at all. He shouts when she does not eat all her food, he shouts when she eats it too fast. He shouts when she cries, he shouts when she laughs loud. Still later, she learns the meaning of his shouts—he seems to be angry at her all the time, and she does not know why. She looks to her mother for an explanation, but she has none. She just stands by like a witness. She remembers vaguely when her sister was born, but remembers clearly that her father was now shouting at her even more, as if he were angry at her for the birth of her sister.

She gets to be school age and notices that her father does not shout at anybody else but her. He seems to ignore Teresa altogether and issues orders to mother, but he does not shout at either. Christine is ordered to spend all her time after school with her mother, to learn how to cook, clean, do the laundry, put up preserves. She is to grow up to be a "proper wife and mother and you can't start too young." Playing with schoolmates is forbidden, she can only play with Teresa, who is too young to play with. A lot of her time is spent on looking after Teresa, who is whiny and demanding, but it is no use complaining about her to mother. She tells Christine to do her complaining to father, but she does not want to do that. It will only lead to shouting, and now that she is older, she knows that the shouting contains many curse words like "goddam it," and "shit," and she is often greeted with "Here comes the little bitch." When she tries to use these words herself, she is punished. She hates being locked in her room, it is excruciatingly boring. She daydreams a lot about other places, other parents, gleaned from story books and television. She decides that her life will be different, very different, when she grows up.

She is punished in many different ways. Sometimes she has to stand in the corner, facing the wall for an hour. Sometimes she is made to kneel in the corner on raw cobs of corn, harder than stone. Also, her fingertips are hit with a ruler, and worst of all, she has to spend an hour in an airless, dark closet. Teresa is never punished; her father ignores her, and Christine wishes she were Teresa.

She is in her early teens now, in junior high, and she hears a lot about other parents. Some girls claim their fathers are "pussycats," others say they are "a drag." Few complain about being shouted at and punished all the time; maybe sometimes they are, but at other times their fathers are "lovey-dovey." She begins to read novels, mostly Dickens and Thackeray and Austen, and finds that fathers are powerful everywhere. They may not always exercise power, but they hold it in their hands. Christine decides she wants to be powerful.

Christine notices boys and they notice her, mainly because she is the smartest one in the class. Her parents do not seem to be excited because she is a straight-A student, but somehow she knows that it is important to be smart. Her father says, "Hm . . ." when she brings home her report card and does not shout at her or punish. She senses that smartness will be her salvation.

A boy asks her out and she asks her mother if she can go. She refers her to father, who says no. She is too young to date, there will be time enough for that after she graduates from high school. She has dates on the sly and begins to lie at home. Nothing happens on her dates; she holds hands and gets away with lying for a while. Then one day her father sees her walking with a boy hand in hand as he is driving home from work. He stops the car, runs over to her, jerks her away from the boy and pushes her into the car. He yells at the mortified boy to stay away from his daughter and drives her home in enraged silence. From now on, she must be home exactly twenty minutes after school lets out; it takes that long to go the distance. Dire, unspeakable punishments are hinted at if she disobeys.

She already knows that "getting into trouble" means pregnancy, and she makes it her business to find out about it. She uses the school library and the town library and becomes the class expert on contraception. She is determined never to get pregnant. In the town library she meets an older boy who works there. She is fifteen, he eighteen, and she longs for a boy for the first time. He waits for her in the morning just around the corner from her house and walks her to school. After school, whenever he can, he walks her within a block of home, using different routes.

She tells him about her father's tyranny and he suggests that she sneak out of the house after he is asleep. It is dangerous and exciting, and after some hesitation she does it on a moonless night. They go behind the toolshed in the backyard and there is passionate fumbling and grabbing. He wants her then and there, and so does she want him, but manages to ask if he has "protection." He tells her not to worry and tries to go ahead, but she stops him. She will go no further without protection, although he says it is no fun with it. She sends him away and he promises to come back the next night.

He comes back and she makes sure he is protected before she abandons control. She finds the experience painful and messy, and blames the boy for it. She decides he is too inexperienced and stops seeing him; she now knows she needs an older man with plenty of experience with women. Also, she wants to take her time about it the next time. She will have to wait, she knows, until she has left home, but also begins to fantasize about her father's death. Her fantasies are very detailed, they begin with the first sign of what is to be a long, lingering, fatal illness. He comes home from work, paler than usual, having no appetite. Or he notices a pimple that would not go away. Or he gets shot by another hunter and all efforts to save him are to no avail. After fifteen operations he dies. She sees herself sitting by his bed as he is dying; impatiently she waits, counting the minutes on her watch. She sees him signaling to her to come closer; he wants to say something, something that is important to him, but she pretends not to understand. He tries again and she leaves the room. When she comes back, he is dead.

As Christine nears graduation, it is made clear to her that she is expected to go to work immediately, but she is applying for college scholarships without telling her parents, using the address of her best friend. She knows that the biggest struggle of her life is about to take place, a struggle she must not lose. She gets several offers of scholarship and chooses the best school, although it is not the best offer economically. She is planning to work all summer before college in the city where it is located, to save money and to become familiar with her future surroundings. She will also have to have at least one part-time job at college.

She confronts her father with the facts at the last possible minute before leaving. He is enraged, and for the first time ever he strikes her in the face. How dare she sneak around behind his back, making plans for her career! How dare she think she can finish college and become a business executive, of all things! He had secretly nurtured the hope that she might become a stewardess with a major airline, he reveals. "Isn't being a stewardess good enough for you?"

She runs out of the house and leaves on the first bus without her luggage. Hard times ahead. She does not save much during the summer and turns to her uncle the master mechanic for help. He has always been kind to her and obviously disapproved of how she was treated by his brother. He is childless and able to help. She pledges to repay every penny, and in the years to come she does.

College proves to be interesting; she studies hard and gets top grades. Has an affair with a married associate professor of physics, which is very satisfying and exciting. They meet in a motel away from campus and never talk about the future. She learns that she does not need to love men and has a series of affairs through her college years, always with experienced men. There is no contact with her father, but she corresponds with mother and uncle, and occasionally with Teresa. Her sister writes about how disconsolate father has been since Christine left. He comes home from work late and pays no attention to anybody.

She works every summer and manages to get through college, summa cum laude, already accepted by one of the leading business schools in the country. She wants an MBA and an important career. After finishing near the top of her class, she accepts the most promising job offer, moves around a few times, and reaches her present prominence in seven years. Her ambition is to become the first woman president of a major corporation that is not related to fashion and cosmetics.

On the rare occasions she is visiting at home, her father skulks around and says little. His only concerns appear to be whether she has plans for marriage and what her income is. Her indifference toward marriage infuriates him, but he does not let on; her income appalls him. He cannot believe the fact that his daughter is making twice what he is—a woman less than half his age! Other members of her family are in awe of her, and her uncle, who has helped her out, is visibly proud of himself as well.

Christine does not show open anger for her father. She has even considered the possibility that it was his tyranny, his anger at her, that fuelled her ambition and desire, and points at her "placid housewife of a sister" for proof. Teresa was not subjected to father's repression and anger, and since she lacks all ambition, it is possible to Christine that the two are related. She thinks her attitude toward men might have turned out differently had he been a different sort of a father, but does not really believe that it would have been all to the good. She does not see herself as neurotic and considers all her needs to be satisfied for now, nor does she doubt that her career goals will be achieved.

Teresa is now twenty-seven; she married right after high school and has three children, one of them a boy, the apple of grandfather's eye. She lives ten minutes from her parents' house and drops by every day. Her husband works at the same plant her father does, and the two men get along famously. They stop for a few beers together after work and go on hunting and fishing trips whenever they can.

Teresa's recollections of her father during her childhood and teens are entirely different from Christine's. Teresa remembers virtually nothing about him during her first six years; her life revolved around her mother, but she was well aware that father was the ultimate authority in the household. All decisions that went beyond planning the evening meal were in his hands, and since mother seemed satisfied with the arrangement, so was Teresa.

She began to notice early on that her father was paying much attention to Christine. He was asking her a lot of questions all the time and often got angry at her. Teresa did not understand why, but she was secretly glad that Christine was bearing the brunt of father's ire. She was quite content to stay close to mother and avoid questions and yelling. Unlike Christine, she genuinely enjoyed doing household chores, helping mother to market, cook, and clean, and had little interest in school work. Her marks were much worse than Christine's, but her parents did not make anything of it. On one occasion in the third grade, her father said, "Your sister is the smart one in the family, but you are the pretty one," after looking at her report card. This made Teresa happy; being smart seemed to cause questions and trouble, being pretty was simple.

When she was asked if she thought her father was much

more demanding with Christine than with her, and if so, why, Teresa said that it was Christine's smartness that was causing all the problems for her father. She believed that he wanted a son for his first child and made Christine pay for his disappointment; he treated Christine much the same way he would have treated a son. She claims she was never jealous of her sister for drawing so much of her father's attention; she felt safer being with her mother anyway.

Teresa had no problems of any kind, ever. She went steady with one boy only, and married him. They have a good marriage and the children are all well behaved. She is leaving her son pretty much for his father to bring up, and she is treating her daughters in the manner she was treated by her mother. They enjoy hanging around the kitchen, helping her, and the boy, just entering school, already shows signs of becoming a good athlete. She is quite proud of Christine's accomplishments, but does not think she will ever marry, which makes her sorry. For Teresa, a good marriage is still the greatest success a woman can have.

Ralph believes he has done well by his daughters, considering that he had expected to have sons and was unprepared to live with "a houseful of women." His tone is wistful when he speaks of Christine, as if he were wishing to have another chance with her. He is seemingly proud of her, although he admits to failing to understand why a woman would want to live in a man's world and do a man's work. He is also at a loss to explain where she "got her smarts from," and is convinced that Christine would be happier if she was less smart and "more like a woman."

He was asked if he treated his daughters differently and he readily admitted that he had. Confirming Teresa's perception, he said that the shock of having a daughter lasted a long time, and meanwhile he was "probably" treating Christine as if she had been a son. Ralph believes that men expect more from their sons than they do from daughters, and he "probably" expected more from Christine than he did from Teresa. He does not think he was too hard on her, but if he was, it was entirely for her sake. When he was asked why he thought they were not close today, he said that Christine apparently rejected him when he opposed her going to college and has still not forgiven him. He felt it was up to her to make the first move toward a better relationship but stated quite clearly that he regretted nothing. He would still oppose college, despite Christine's success; he is convinced she will end up as a lonely old woman without a husband and children, and no amount of success or money can compensate for that.

Ralph has nothing but praise for Teresa. She has never given him a bit of trouble and turned out to be a "real woman," just like her mother; besides, she has given him the grandson he always wanted. Asked to speculate if Teresa would have turned out differently had she been treated as Christine was, his reply was no. Just as Christine was born with her "smarts," so was Teresa with her "womanliness," and in the end, both would have turned out as they did, regardless of how they had been treated.

Ralph is a guardian of old-time working-class values and he has no problems with sorting out things. Hard work is extolled, and the rights and responsibilities of men and women are clearly defined. They are not permitted to trespass on each other's territory, and if they do, they should expect proper punishment.

It was Ralph's cross to bear in life that he had two daughters and no sons. He was totally unprepared for the situation and could only respond with anger; although he claims to have accepted the facts while the girls were still very young, the evidence shows that he did not. In Ralph's world, the only acceptable roles for women are those of wife and mother, and if he turned his anger on Christine it was because he would have expected so much more from a firstborn son than he could reasonably get from a firstborn daughter. All there was for Christine to do was to grow up to be a good wife/mother, which left him with nothing to do.

Ralph's anger expressed itself in tyranny which spent itself on Christine and spared Teresa, and Christine responded by rejecting the expectations attached to her and creating her own. In a sense, she took charge of her own life early on and forged ahead indomitably and successfully. She chose to sacrifice home life and stable sex, and in rejecting her father she rejected all men as principal players in her life.

Teresa found the expectations she bore to her liking and fulfilled them with a smile. She carries Ralph's values forward into another generation.

Brian is an accountant in his mid-thirties with a prosperous practice in the Southwest. He has three children—all boys—between the ages of five and ten, and, to all appearances, is happily married. He is the most devoted of fathers, spending all of his available time with his sons, and often forgoing business in order to take them to a baseball game or the circus. He has given careful thought to their future and is ready to make all necessary sacrifices to ensure that they will receive the best possible education. He is firm with them but not strict, openly affectionate but not spoiling. He always keeps his promises to them and never makes any he knows he cannot keep.

Brian's sister, Nicole, is in her late twenties and lives in the West. She is married to a professional man in his early forties and has chosen not to have a career of her own, even though they are not going to have children. Their marriage appears to be exceedingly happy, and by her own account it is "perfect." She spends much of her time as a hospital volunteer and helping out in drug rehabilitation programs, but is always home in time to greet her husband when he comes home from work. When she is asked why she does not want to have children, she replies that she is afraid to. In fact, she says, she is not having children for the same reason her brother did have them, except that Brian had the courage to confront and conquer his fears while she does not. They had both seen what parents can do to children, for their father was a tyrant who brutalized his wife and children, and when Nicole and Brian had grown up, he committed suicide.

They have made an extensive effort after his death to find out as much as they could about his background, about which they had known nothing. They had an almost morbid curiosity to learn what had gone into making him what he was, as they knew him. They sought out his relatives, colleagues, and friends, and talked with them at length. The picture that emerged was not at all what they had expected.

Their father, Bruce, was a third-generation scholar of ancient Greek, a full professor by the time he was thirty. By all accounts, he was rigorous but not tyrannical, regarded as an excellent teacher by his students and peers. He had a reputation for turning out students who were really well versed in his subject and maintained enthusiasm for it even after they left school. According to surviving relatives, he was strictly brought up—strictly but justly, as a cousin of his put it. He seemed to have admired his father and needed no push to follow in his footsteps. Nothing could be learned about his marriage to a compliant woman of excellent family beyond the tangible facts. They led a very private life, and while they accepted an occasional social invitation, they were never known to issue one. Nicole and Brian could find no one who had been a guest in their house or who knew anything about the nature of their marriage. Nicole and Brian were sole witnesses.

On one point, all who had known Bruce agreed. About a year after his marriage, he was drafted into service early in World War II, and was soon captured by the Japanese. He spent the rest of the war in various prison camps where the survivor rate was approximately 10 percent and had been subjected to all sorts of barbarous tortures. All the men who were captured with him were killed or died of illnesses and malnutrition, and when he was liberated in 1945, he weighed ninety pounds. He did not speak about his experiences to anyone beyond the bare outlines of his story, but he was visibly affected by them. He was always tall and slender, and now he became gaunt and haunted-looking, and his once ramrod bearing was bent. He was never talkative, but now he was almost a recluse, attending only to his duties as a teacher.

The memories of Brian and Nicole are so similar that they could be fused without distortion. Ever since they can remember, which in Brian's case goes back to the crib, they found him "menacing." The moment he entered the house, usually in midafternoon, he demanded his tea and toast, and if it was not forthcoming immediately, he cursed his wife unmercifully and savagely, disregarding the presence of the children. His curses were delivered in a loud, precisely enunciated tone, and they were extremely elaborate. As the children grew older, they learned that they included not only commonplace curse words, but also obsolete Elizabethan phrases, intermingled with Greek and Japanese curses. If he noticed the children, his cursing would be extended to include them, after which they would be banished from the room. If they did not move instantly, he would leap at them, beat them with his fists, and kick them as they retreated, cursing all the while.

All their memories of father were related to his brutality. They were ordered to do this and that, and if they failed to do it, or even hesitated, they would be beaten. His blows lacked power, fortunately for them, on account of his frailness, but they were delivered with such vehemence, such amazing quickness, that they were invariably frightening. Even when they were teenagers and could have easily resisted him, they were powerless, paralyzed with fear.

Their mother was totally submissive and complaisant, and often admonished them not to anger father, because "he suffered so much in the war." The implications of that statement were so vast that they did not dare to question it until they were much older. They found little protection from mother, and they learned to protect each other. They were very close and their alliance represented some sort of defiance, even if open resistance was out of the question. They would often take the blame for each other, which "felt good."

By the time Brian was in his mid-teens and Nicole a couple of years younger, they were both physically stronger than father, and he must have realized the almost comic absurdity of his flailing at them, even though their fear of him was undiminished. He ceased physical abuse and increased the dosage and intensity of verbal castigations. Everything they did or did not do aroused his ire and opened the floodgates; less than perfect marks in school, tardiness, noisiness, unkempt appearance—anything could become provocation for him. Nicole never even attempted to bring boys into the house when she was old enough to do so, and her dating had to be conducted under the veil of elaborate fabrications, fronted by Brian. His extracurricular activities gave him enough latitude to cover up his own dates.

They never spoke about father to anyone. He was a shared secret, hidden to outsiders like a vice. Between them, he was the subject of frequent discussion and analysis; their fear of him remained constant until the day he died, but the hatred they felt in early childhood later turned into a combination of loathing and pity. They often fantasized about his captivity during the war and savored his imagined suffering of the tortures they concocted for him. One of Nicole's favorites was forcing a thin, long glass tube up his penis, and when it was all inside, shattering it with a blow to the penis. Brian created an all-powerful mandarin in China who responded only to Brian's wishes; all he had to do was push a button and the mandarin would bring about father's destruction. He never pushed the button, but its secret existence gave him vast unexercised power.

Nicole and Brian agree that neither could have survived growing up as an only child without serious psychological damage; they identify strongly with the brother-sister pair in Cocteau's *Les Enfants Terribles* in terms of the strength of their bond which enabled them to grow up relatively unscathed. When father killed himself, Brian was twenty-four and Nicole twenty-one; she felt relieved, he indifferent.

When mother died shortly thereafter of a longstanding cancer, they both felt a certain amount of guilt. They should have made an effort, they believed, to relieve her of the anguish she must have endured living with father. But had she really suffered at his hand? They did not know, could not know.

Brian and Nicole are convinced that their father was irreparably damaged by his captivity during the war and consider that as the irrefutable explanation for his behavior toward them. They cite cases from the literature of psychology of concentration camp survivors who learned by necessity to identify with their tormentors and in later life displayed brutality and tyranny. This enables Brian and Nicole to forgive him to a certain extent, more and more as time goes on.

There is little to be said here, as information on Brian and Nicole's father is scant, yet their belief in the "irrefutability" of the cause of his brutality is suspect. To the question, Would his behavior have been the same if he had not experienced the horrors of Japanese concentration camps?—one hesitates to answer with an unqualified no. First, there is the matter of his isolation from the world before the war, of which nothing is known, but which may well be related to his later brutality. Why did they not have visitors? Did he perhaps beat his wife?

Second and foremost, the thesis about the brutality of some concentration camp survivors does not hold up to scrutiny. True, many inmates identified with their tormentors and engaged in cruel behavior while in camp, but there is no evidence that they carried over this behavior into normal life. Many such assumptions about concentration camp survivors, notably, the belief in their guilt feelings, have become truisms without solid evidence.

The opposite ways in which Brian and Nicole resolved

their nightmares are striking, especially as both seem to be successful so far. Choosing to confront fears can have the same consequence as choosing not to confront them.

idealized

Michael is in his late seventies, confined to a wheelchair by arthritis but still exuding mental vigor. He is one of a rare breed—a retired politician—and his memories come forth clearly and quickly, summoned up and related with relish. He is eager to declare that he has had a good life in every way, with much to be proud of, and has no cause for shame. Values and habits acquired in childhood stood him in good stead throughout his life—he has never had reason to question their soundness—and he has passed them on to his only son, firm in the belief that the passage of a generation could not have weakened their hold. Indeed, as Michael sees it, his son, Edward, grew up to be "a man of solid substance," "a perfect son," although Michael declines to take any credit for it. He attributes his own success and satisfaction in life, which includes Edward's success and satisfaction, to his father.

Michael was the youngest of four children of a county judge, known statewide to all as "Judge Ben," and his wife, Lucy, daughter of a dairy farmer. Judge Ben's forebears have lived in the state for generations and his father had distinguished himself as an officer in the Civil War. The family has always lived by values derived from the Good Book, wedded to intense patriotism and a bit of xenophobia, and no black sheep has ever darkened its annals. Everything was clear and above board; the rules were spelled out, laid down, and passed on by the elders, and they were learned, understood, and accepted by the young, generation after generation. A third cousin, Michael admits, married a Jewish engineer back around 1910 without the family's permission and moved to a distant city. Yet "even she" had known the rules, and the branch of the family she sprouted turned out to be "fertile, God-fearing, productive stock."

Michael's mother spent most of her life in the kitchen and played virtually no role in her children's upbringing. She was present at meals and always accessible, but all decisions were made by Judge Ben, and her role was at most that of an intermediary. She could be relied on for solace and succor in cases of minor physical and psychological injury, but matters more important than a scraped knee or a mild rebuke from a teacher fell under Judge Ben's jurisdiction.

Michael, his two brothers and sisters were all born at one-year intervals and grew up an exceptionally closely knit bunch. They went to the same schools from first grade to senior high, and usually left together in the morning and came home together in the early afternoon. The leisurely pace of the small-town county court enabled Judge Ben to be home by the time the children returned from school and from then till bedtime he devoted his time to them completely. The routine varied very little. He sat with them while they were having their after-school snack, discussing the events of the day, both at school and at the courthouse. He would then spend a half hour or so with each child in his study, starting with the oldest, ending with Michael, the youngest. At these sessions, the child's particular problems, accomplishments, and hopes were reviewed in detail, advice, approbation, or censure meted out, and the Judge's philosophy of life mused upon in brief installments.

To Michael, these sessions with the Judge were the highlights of growing up. They were the most important part of the day, and he cannot recall a single instance when he felt disappointed or let down. Michael is the only surviving child, and he maintains that all the children felt the same way and hardly a day went by when they did not have some sort of affectionate talk about the Judge, exchanging notes on what each of them had learned from him that day. He recollects no incidents of rivalry among the children, because none of them detected any sign of favoritism and the time spent by the Judge with each child was scrupulously equal. Saturdays, which were mostly devoted to fishing, in which the Judge was famously expert, he took the children with him in alternate twos. By the time Michael was six, he was as skilled in fishing streams and rivers as any grown-up, and it remained his principal diversion until arthritis compelled him to give it up.

When Michael's oldest brother decided in his teens that he no longer cared to go fishing every Saturday, he was not pressured to change his mind, nor did the Judge comment on his defection to the other children. It was quite clear to them all from the beginning that the Judge was their loving guide and mentor, their instructor in the theory and practice of life, but it was no less clear that dissent and the choice of other alternatives was not ruled out. This is not to say that the Judge would have tolerated serious deviations from the norms, but the children's individual likes and dislikes were allowed to flourish. For example, when Michael's sister had a brief but intense flirtation with atheism during her teens, the Judge spent endless hours showing her the errors of her way by summoning up every theological and philosophical argumentation he could muster. At the same time, it was unmistakably clear that had she persisted in her folly in the face of the evidence of righteousness, she would have been compelled to choose between family and banishment. On the other hand, personal preferences, such as refusal to go fishing or, in Michael's case, a particular fondness of girls, were not interfered with.

The Judge's rules of life were quite simple and undemanding. Moral behavior was derived entirely from biblical models, with no room for any sort of compromise. Love of country had unquestionable priority over individual preferences or even family life. Marriage and children were taken for granted, and any alternative for them would have been unacceptable. Above and beyond these boundaries, which the Judge regarded as spacious enough for virtuous happiness, the children were expected and encouraged to pursue socially and patriotically beneficial careers, and the Judge lived long enough to see his expectations spectacularly fulfilled. His oldest son became a minister and died a bishop, the second son chose journalism and went on to write nationally syndicated conservative political commentaries, and his daughter became headmistress of a religiously oriented private girls' school. They all married and had children, lived spotless lives, and revered the Judge for as long as he lived, as long as they lived.

Michael, who is now older than his father got to be, still speaks of him admiringly and is rueful on one subject only: He wishes that the Judge's views on sex had been broader than they were. He feels that all the children, he in particular, were adversely affected by the Judge's narrow interpretation of sexual conduct, which was based on the Old Testament but also influenced by old wives' tales and unidentifiable prejudices. He was not satisfied with proscribing premarital sex on biblical grounds but found it necessary to reinforce the ban by invoking the spectre of venereal diseases. According to him, it was a virtual certainty that premarital and extramarital sex would infect one with one form or another of VD, and an absolute certainty if one's partner in such a carnal sin were of another race.

Michael admits to having lusted for girls and women as far back as he can remember and to having struggled mightily against his natural impulses in his youth. He feels that the energy and time expended on his internal conflicts were inordinate and could have been better used, for most of his teen years were spent in a state of "moral exhaustion." Decades later, he found out that his brothers were similarly plagued, and his sister's husband once confided in him to the point of saying that she considered sex as an imposition.

He is proud of the fact that he did not inhibit his own son in sexual matters, yet does not blame his father for having inhibited him and attributes it to generational differences. He married as early as he could to put an end to his turmoil and has had no occasion to regret it.

Michael decided early on to follow in his father's footsteps in his choice of career. He planned on first becoming a lawyer, earning a good reputation, getting involved in politics, and running for a judgeship in the state. Eventually, if all went well, he could envision himself on the bench of a federal court. The early phases came about as planned and he became a member of the state legislature before he was thirty. He was a loyal member of his party and was easily reelected twice. The usual temptations of political life left him untouched—conflicts of interest, campaign fund abuses, payoffs, malfeasances of office, did not mark him. He was so effective a legislator, with a reputation so pure, that the party leadership moved to put his name up to be considered for a federal district judgeship when he was thirty-four, and his father still a county judge.

Honored as he felt by this unexpected development, Michael went into a state of panic. At first, he thought that his symptoms—pounding heart, sweating, bad dreams, extreme anxiety—were a reaction to the probability that he was to be appointed to a job for which he felt unprepared. It was his wife who hinted at the possibility that his feelings may have more to do with his father than with his qualifications for the job, and after some thought he came to see that she was right. His father had reacted to the news with great enthusiasm and pride, but now Michael decided to discuss the matter with him once more. It was on a Wednesday that they decided to have lunch Monday next to talk things over. Sunday night, the Judge died in his sleep.

Even before grief had a chance to overcome him, Michael sent word to the powers that be that he did not wish to be considered for the appointment to the federal bench. He did it without even thinking, he did it as an unconscious reflex. It took many years of reflection for Michael to realize why he had done what he had done and to be able to see things in full context. When he talks about it today, his voice is thinner than it is usually, his eyes gaze into the distance, and he speaks slowly and reflectively. He speaks of his then unconscious realization that accepting the nomination would have raised him above his father, made him more important—a position unthinkable for him to assume. He is certain that even if he had had the opportunity to discuss the matter with the Judge and receive his repeated proud endorsement—and he feels sure he would have—even then, he would not have been able to accept the appointment. He admits that if the opportunity arose later in his life, after his father's death, he would have been proud and honored to accept it. It would then have been a fulfillment of the Judge's expectations of him, and he would have been certain of his posthumous approval.

Michael concentrated on his political career after his father's death and served for two decades as speaker of the state assembly. He remained as virtuous in politics as he was in his private life, and retired in his seventies with honors heaped upon him from all sides. He brought up his only son, Edward, by the precepts of the Judge, except for being more "liberal" in sexual matters. He is too modest to say so, but it is clear that he feels as revered and admired by his son as he revered and admired his father.

Edward is in his late forties, in his "prime," as he likes to put it—a captain of industry, yet brimming with ambition. He tends to agree with his father's assessment of their relationship, although there are aspects to his life that he keeps from the old man. His upbringing was very similar to that of his father's, except that Michael had considerably less time to spend with Edward than the Judge had spent with him. Politics is a time-consuming business and Michael was on the stump a great deal of the time. Nevertheless, he always made himself accessible to his son and would interrupt important meetings to take a phone call from him or to see him if he dropped by.

Edward had known his paternal grandmother and notes that his own mother was a "carbon copy" of her, both in physical appearance and in the role she played in family life.

She took very good care of her only son and her household, but the boy learned soon enough that his father was the arbiter in matters of any importance. Each evening, during and after dinner, he received his father's complete attention and would invariably get a phone call from him whenever he was out of town. Never at any time did Edward feel that his father was absent or unavailable.

During their time together, Michael put distinct emphasis on the importance of ambition and achievement. It was evident to Edward that his father resented his wife's inability to bear more children, and he became aware at a very young age that he bore the weighty responsibility of attaining Michael's expectations. Unlike many only children, especially boys, who react adversely to paternal expectations, Edward flourished on responsibility; its weight was not a burden but a bounty to be harvested. Pleasing his father was a stimulant to him, and he would set goals to be attained voluntarily and give achievements to Michael as a bouquet.

Edward never questioned the values his father transmitted to him, even though he was taunted in high school and college for his rock-ribbed conservatism. In fact, the older he got, the more conservative he became, and the wealthier he became, the more he spent on and donated to conservative causes, be they political or spiritual. He says he tried his best to convey his beliefs to his five children and thinks he succeeded by and large, "considering the times we live in." Three of his children were old enough to vote in 1980, and all voted for Reagan. He has qualms about his eighteen-year-old daughter, who is a "radical feminist or feminist radical," but believes that she is just going through a phase.

Edward is very proud of being the first wealthy person in the history of his family, although he speaks glowingly about the public service accomplishments of his father and grandfather. When the time came for him to choose a career, his father advised him to try his hand in one of the then budding industries, such as plastics, electronics, or computers, and Edward gladly took the advice. He has amassed substantial wealth in electronics and considers it his duty to contribute generously to public service causes. It is one of his ambitions that at least two of his children should devote their careers to "good works"—a favorite phrase of his father's.

Edward seemed eager to bring up the subject of sex. His father began talking about it when Edward was a teenager and made it quite clear, repeatedly so, that he wished his own father had spent more time on the subject. He ruefully told his son that he was never able to "indulge" himself, because his father had made sexual matters unpalatable and sinful, and he wanted to be sure not to make the same mistake with his own son. In Edward's recollection, this was the only time that Michael made a critical remark about his father.

Michael encouraged him to seek out sexual experiences as a way of preparing himself for marriage, because he had learned that when both partners are inexperienced, the marriage will be arid. At the same time, he emphasized the importance of marrying a virgin, allowing for no alternative in that matter. Similarly, masturbation was ruled out on biblical grounds. Edward was advised to avail himself of the services of "loose women," a designation wide enough to include prostitutes, divorcées, certain widows, and "wild girls." Seduction of "innocent Christian girls" was inadmissible.

On his sixteenth birthday, Edward traveled fifty-seven miles by bus to the nearest town that accommodated lusty travelers and followed the directions of a schoolmate to a local bordello. He had only the vaguest notions of what to expect and was accordingly nervous. As he approached, he saw a man come out of the house, sit down on the stoop, and proceed to tie his shoelaces. The scene shocked Edward so that he turned on his heels and headed back to the bus terminal. What could be taking place in there that required the removal of one's shoes? He was mortified at the thought of such intimacy and several months went by before he could summon up enough fortitude to become informed on such questions.

He was eventually initiated through the graciousness of a "wild girl" in town and found the experience so exhilarating that he sought to repeat it as frequently as he could. At first, he reported his accomplishments to his father to obtain his confirmation and approval, but he discerned that the subject did not sit comfortably with him and he soon stopped. From that time on, his intimacy with his father stopped short of the subject of sex, a development that has made Edward feel guilty. He deeply regrets that his father has never enjoyed a satisfactory sex life while he himself has a very good one. Unlike Michael, whose sex life was inhibited by his father's strictures, Edward finds great pleasure in sexual activity; sometimes he feels that his enjoyment is in fact enhanced by his father's deprivation, as if he experienced it for him by proxy.

As he got older, Edward interpreted the definition of "loose women" more and more broadly, and he now holds that any woman who makes herself available is "loose," even if she is married or a virgin. Consequently, he abandoned the tenet of marital fidelity without even feeling hypocritical about it. He justifies his position by declaring abiding loyalty to his wife and by restricting his infidelities to business trips. As he puts it, he does it on his "own time," taking away nothing from his wife. He has never had a liaison of any duration and would not consider having one, because then he would have to lie and sneak around and become a hypocrite.

When Edward is asked what his father would think about his reinterpretation of old rules, he has a ready answer. While he feels justified and righteous about his sexual conduct, he has two reasons for not wanting his father to know about it. First, Michael belongs to a generation whose rules are inflexible and unchanging; second, Edward feels guilty about experiencing the pleasures denied to his father. Not guilty enough to change, but guilty enough to not want to hurt his feelings.

There is still another subject excluded from the intimacy of father and son, and it causes Edward greater anguish than anything else in his life. As he was growing prosperous and powerful, he discovered that when viewed from the perspective of morality, the conduct of business, certainly successful business, contained impure, even corrupt, practices.

Certain arrangements had to be made in order to obtain contracts in certain places, money often had to change hands under tables, favors had to be granted and received. All this was against Edward's grain, as it would have been against Michael's and the Judge's, yet he was committed to the accumulation of wealth and power with the blessing of his father. In real terms, he had no choice—he had to be successful and do what was required. In moral terms, his father's approval of the entirety of his enterprise implied approval of its details.

Edward is aware of the ethical dubiety of his formula, but he has learned to live with it. His anguish derives from the conviction that his father would not be able to accept it and endorse his impure practices, and he finds release only in his generous support of what he and his father regard as good causes. He has also exercised great care in guiding his children in such a way that they should be aware of the corruptions of this world yet have the moral strength to resist them. He does not want any of them to choose business as a career, and so far none of them has any such interests.

For a variety of reasons, Edward's children—three sons and two daughters—were not available for intensive talks about their father, but they did speak of him at some length. Monroe, the oldest—all the children's names begin with M, after Michael—is twenty-five, in his last year of study for the ministry. He is not effusive, but it is clear that he holds his father in awe. He recalls his childhood as having been "ordinary," and credits Edward for guiding him toward the spiritual life. He wants to marry soon after receiving his ministry because he is eager to experience fatherhood, which he regards as the "highest vocation."

Michelle, next in line, is twenty-three, a second-year law student. She has strong intellectual views, including the belief that conservatism as an ideology is just coming into its own and that her father's philosophy will become prevalent in her lifetime. She intends to work in law to that end, but she is not yet sure about what form her work will take. She recalls having always been proud of her father—in grade school because he was the youngest father in school, in high school because he was handsome, and now because he is "fervent and committed."

Mark is twenty-one, fresh out of college, intent on entering the Foreign Service. He is laconic and volunteers no information, answering questions in monosyllables. The only subject that warms him up is America; he is intensely patriotic and expects that he will be able to effect changes in the country's image abroad. His only concern is that his father's conservative reputation, which he fully endorses, will keep him out of the "old boys' network," retarding his progress.

Mike is twenty, still in college, undecided about the future. He is the only one in the family who has an obvious sense of humor. He recalls his childhood as having been "a lot of fun," but, unlike his older siblings, he allows himself to be critical of his father. He thinks the old man is "a bit windy," although he respects him for standing up for his beliefs, for "putting his money where his mouth is." Mike has no political beliefs of any kind and hopes that he never will, but does not judge his father for his views. He clearly likes Edward, but does not take him as seriously as the other children do.

Maria is eighteen, the only one of the five who causes Edward concern. She is a fervent feminist, a political radical of the leftist persuasion. She was the only child to insist on not attending the family college and entering a serious-minded women's college in the East. Still a freshman, she has already made herself known on campus, both to students and faculty. She thinks that her family has been reactionary for generations, although she does not put the blame personally on her father, grandfather, or anyone in particular. She believes they meant well but were "miseducated." She is proud to be the first woman in the family to have come out of the kitchen and bedroom, and entertains the notion of not marrying. Despite her grave philosophical and political differences with her father, she appears to like him as a person, and the prospect of breaking off relations with him in the future makes her profoundly unhappy though no less committed to her beliefs.

Edward professes not to have a favorite child, but he appears to be more intense when talking about his daughters and more analytical when talking about his sons. He turns almost passionate in enumerating Michelle's virtues and in expressing concern over Maria's views, while his pride in Monroe's "spiritual strength," in Mark's "political acumen," in Mike's "artistic nature," is conveyed with reserve. He is most emotional, almost tearful, when he talks about how proud and happy his father is about his grandchildren, as if that were the most important aspect of his own fatherhood.

Fathers are often idealized, even when they are far from being ideal from an objective point of view. Interestingly, the tendency to idealize seems to get passed on from father to child, and the traits that constitute the magnet of idealization seem to remain constant from generation to generation. The Judge's religiosity, conservatism, patriotism, and biblical morality passed virtually undiluted to his four children, to be passed on by Michael to his son Edward, who, for the sake of expediency, subjected these precepts to certain reinterpretations but maintained full faith in them. In the third generation, at least three of Edward's children continue the tradition, while two others may or may not.

To be a good father requires a talent that cannot be learned, treatises on "fathering" to the contrary notwithstanding. While it is relatively easy to fake or manipulate modulations of feelings among adults, whether in the act of conveyance or of acceptance, it is utterly impossible to do so with children. Children are not only artless but also have perfect pitch; they detect complacence or inconstancy of feeling in adults in a flash. By the same token, when children idealize a parent, one can be absolutely certain that the magnet of idealization is true and real in the parent. Objective observers may regard the trait or traits that constitute it unworthy, despicable, or merely indifferent, but to the idealizing child it is the representation of a real need, even a yearning, that must be embraced, seized, and revered.

The idealized parent is a parent with a talent for being a parent. The Judge was certainly a father with talent, even genius. To be a father seems to have been his main calling in life, and he devoted himself to it wholeheartedly. He was generously affectionate, completely attentive, constant in feeling and character, wise and reliable as guide and mentor. All four of his children tuned in on the genuineness of his beliefs and convictions and adopted them as the main themes of their own lives.

That the Judge should have planted erroneous and eventually harmful notions about sex in his children's minds was a predictable consequence of his biblical morality, and for that very reason his children apparently did not blame him. They were without rancor, as if the frustrated aspect of their lives had been dealt to them by God. In the same vein, Michael attached no significance to the timing of the Judge's death, even if psychologically sophisticated observers might have deemed it an act of supreme hostility.

In the next generation, Edward's idealization of his father is total and a source of guilt for his failure to live up to paternal standards in some respects. At the same time, his own expectations for his children are relatively diminished because he is more in tune with the ways of the world than were his father and grandfather. In the third generation, the idealization process begins to break down into its components, with one son focusing on his father's spiritual values, one daughter on his political ideology, another son on his patriotism, and two children uncommitted as yet.

In other families, as we shall see, idealization is restricted to one child, unshared by siblings, and in still others, idealized qualities are far from admirable to outsiders.

* * *

Jack is in his early thirties and works in professional sports at the middle-management level. His five-year-old marriage is stable and devoted, and children have been deferred until he is past thirty-five and his wife past thirty. He is a cheerful man who likes to refer to himself as a "jock" and as having a "jock mentality." All his friends are professional athletes, and both he and his wife are avid runners, swimmers, skiers, and tennis players. He likes everything about sports—the noise, the crowds, the presence of media people, the wagering, even the smell of dressing rooms.

Jack's father, Howard, was a professional athlete during the 1940s and 1950s, and while his was not a household name, he always played for top teams and was regarded as a good journeyman player. When he retired, he quickly got a job as a coach and has never been without a job since. He is now in his late sixties, still working and in excellent health. He has been living apart from Jack's mother for some fifteen years, but neither has found it compelling to seek a divorce. Howard loves the sporting life in all its aspects, even the dreary trips on the road to the same towns year after year, and the notion of retirement is totally alien to him. During off-seasons, he takes jobs in Europe and Latin America, coaching foreign teams just to keep his hand in the game. He cannot imagine working at any other occupation. He is very happy to have his son working in the business and telephones him every night, no matter where he is, to discuss sports and to tell him about his amorous adventures.

Jack adores and admires his father, and while his personal life is quite unlike Howard's, he prefers the old man's company to anyone else's. Even today, he takes his problems to Howard, whether professional or personal, and confides in him more than he does in his wife. He readily admits that he would rather spend time with his father than with his wife, even though he loves her completely, because Howard is getting on and "may not be around much longer." He has idealized his father ever since he can remember and he is as proud of it as he is of him.

Jack has a sister, Stephanie, who is only twenty and works as a bartender for the time being. Before that, she had

fathers

traveled with various rock groups as a roadie, and plans to become a songwriter eventually. She also expects to "end up" as a lesbian, because all her relationships with men seem to end "freaky." She has not actually had a lesbian experience yet, but feels ready for it. Stephanie is very fond of Jack, but finds his admiration of their father totally incomprehensible. She thinks Howard is an "old lech" who has never grown up and for whom sports is the only reality. She also thinks that Howard should never have gotten married and had children. She has never met a man who was less qualified for the role of husband and father and feels bitterly resentful at what he has done to her, her mother, and her brother.

Howard sees himself as a devoted father, but he does not claim ever to have been a devoted husband. Aside from having been away from home at least half of the time, he was always a womanizer and never made a secret of it. His father was killed in World War I before he was born, and he was brought up by his mother and two older sisters. Growing up in a household of women agreed with Howard, and he came to expect being pampered and babied by women as an adult. He never had much difficulty in obtaining such treatment, for his athletic prowess attracted women in sufficient numbers from his school years on. As a matter of fact, Howard admits that the attraction of women to jocks was the major factor in his choice of career. He had wanted to be an architect but became so allured with the easy availability of women when he was a high school star athlete that he decided to follow the easier and pleasanter road of the professional athlete.

The only reason Howard got married was his desire to become a father, and he chose his wife solely on the basis of her sexual talents. She was not even interested in sports and never attended the games Howard played in; their only common ground and principal occupation was sex. She did not mind his infidelities on the road, Howard claims, because he kept telling her that she was the best. What she did mind though was his frequent absence, and not long after giving birth to Jack, she began to have infidelities of her own. She did not attempt to conceal her activities from Howard and he did not try to stop her. It was agreed between them that they would be always available to each other when Howard was home, and whatever they did during his absences would be immaterial to their marriage. They did not plan on having any more children after Jack was born, and when she became pregnant with Stephanie a dozen years later, Howard wanted her to have an abortion. She refused, and that was to be the beginning of the end of their marriage.

Howard spent as much time with Jack as he possibly could when he was home, and even spoke to him on the telephone every day when he was on the road. He volunteered the information that his having grown up without a father had a great deal to do with his special efforts at the beginning of his fatherhood, but he grew to love his son so much that all his efforts turned into pleasures. There was nothing he liked better than to have Jack attend the games as soon as he was old enough to know what was going on, and when the boy reached drinking age, he would take him along on his postgame carousing. He is proud of the fact that he introduced Jack to sex and taught him everything he knew about women. He is certain that the boy did not suffer any guilt feelings on account of loyalty to his mother, because he explained to him how things were between them as husband and wife as soon as he judged him to be old enough to understand.

It became evident early on that Jack did not have sufficient athletic skills to compete on the professional level, and as soon as he graduated from high school, Howard got him a job in the front office. It was understood between father and son that Jack's place was in sports and if he could not participate actively, he was going to learn the management side of it. They were virtually inseparable anyway, and now they were in close physical proximity at all times of the day. When the team was at home, they had frequent contact during the working day, and until Jack got married, they also spent most of their free time together. It was not at all unusual for them to double-date on the road, as Jack's job called for him to visit the team on the road from time to time. They took quite a bit of ribbing from players and coaches, but far from minding it, they would have missed it if it had not been forthcoming.

It is a point of pride with Howard to make it clear that he and his son shared more than a few women sexually, sometimes even on the same night. He is certain that this practice did not cause Jack any psychological damage and points to his successful marriage as proof. He is ready to admit that this was unusual behavior between father and son, but then he points out that his relationship with Jack is unusually close and strong enough to support unorthodox practices. He was very happy when Jack decided to settle down and approved of his choice of wife completely. He often plays tennis with his daughter-in-law and the three of them go out for dinner and to nightclubs frequently.

Howard is far less ebullient when the subject of his daughter is brought up, but he is quite willing to confront it. He says he loves Stephanie, or rather that he would love to love her, but she will not let him. True, he did ask his wife to have an abortion after Stephanie was conceived, but once she was born, all that was forgotten. Unfortunately, their marriage was beginning to go bad at about the same time, although Howard does not acknowledge that there may be a link between the two events. It was just that he was "tiring of having to come home to a wife," and as a consequence he saw less of Stephanie than he might have wanted. The girl was about five years old when the parents' estrangement became total, and contact between father and daughter has been intermittent and random for the past fifteen years. Slyly, almost as an aside, he says he was "perhaps too much of a tomcat to have a daughter in the first place."

Jack's first recollection of his father was a state of being rather than a specific event. He remembers a certain tension attached to the feeling of waiting for him, even before he could comprehend the meaning of his presences and absences. He cannot be sure whether he perceived the tension in his mother's behavior and adopted it or if he produced it independently, but he is sure that the pleasant tension of waiting for father was the dominant mood of his childhood and adolescence. As soon as he was able to read and count, he prepared a chart of the schedule of his father's team, so that he could tell at a glance where his father was going to be each day for the next six months. He put large X's over the days of his absences, using a different color crayon for each city.

Jack recalls very clearly that his mother encouraged his special interest in his father's whereabouts and may have even originated the idea for such a chart, but it took him several years to discover her reasons for doing so. Although he was aware that his mother was being visited by a succession of men almost every afternoon—one "uncle" giving way to another every month or so—he developed the curious notion that these uncles were in fact bringing messages from father who was away, confidential messages meant for his mother alone. While he was a little jealous at being excluded, he was at the same time proud, for his father had to be exceptionally powerful to be able to dispatch messengers from distant places.

His bedroom adjoined the parental one and he was long accustomed to certain peculiar sounds next door whenever his father was home. They seemed to be associated with some pleasant activity, and he often forced himself to stay awake and enjoy them. One day, when he was about seven, he was in bed with the measles when he heard the same kind of noises coming from the other bedroom, although his father was out of town. Almost thirty years later, Jack can still recapture the moment of panic and recognition he experienced. After the initial wave of confusion and panic passed over him, suddenly everything fell into place. He knew that mother was doing father wrong, and he knew that the succession of uncles was not one of messengers but one of father's betrayers. He did not know how the betrayal was carried out, he could not imagine the details, yet he knew that wrong had been done.

Jack's discovery caused him great anxiety. Should he tell his father what he has found out or should he conceal it from him and protect him from this terrible knowledge? His father was due back home a week later and, aside from the annoyance of the measles, Jack spent the entire time agonizing over what to do. His decision was made the moment his father entered the room; he knew instantly that it was impossible for him to hurt Howard and that he himself would have to bear the brunt of his mother's betrayal. In recalling the episode, Jack seems to be proud of his decision; for a seven-year-old child, it must have been a severe ordeal to become the guardian of conjugal secrets.

The innate streak of nobility displayed by Jack had its costs in the years to come. His relationship with his mother became constricted and he could never really trust her again—an affliction that was to extend to all women for many years. At the same time, his admiration for his father deepened with every passing year, to the point where he identified with him almost totally. They spent all their available time together, and by the time Jack reached his mid-teens they became not only father and son but buddies, in the gamiest sense of the term.

His mother's behavior must have acted as a propellant of sexual curiosity, for Jack got interested in sex by the time he was eight when he became a habitual masturbator. He was beginning to find out what sex was about, and the sound effects of the parental bedroom acquired visual and tactile dimensions. His father started educating him in sexual manners and mores when he was about ten, and arranged his first assignation before he was thirteen, just after his sister was born. The woman chosen for Jack's initiation was one of the many team followers—what would be called a sports groupie today—and her enthusiasm for the task got him off to a good sexual start. Soon afterward, the estrangement of his parents reached the point where Howard rented a small apartment for himself and came to the house less and less often.

The separation did not affect Jack's relations with his father, because he now spent more time at Howard's apartment than he did at home. By now his interest in everything related to sports was complete, and he could hardly wait to finish school so that he could devote himself to sports professionally. His contact with his mother was minimal, and his sister was much too young to be of any interest to him. In effect, the future course of his life seemed to be set and laid out while he was in his mid-teens.

Jack speaks nostalgically about the fifteen years he spent with his father before he met his wife. He feels that those years not only prepared him for his career but also enabled him to deal with and resolve the problems he had with women, which were created, he feels, by his mother's betrayal. Throughout those years, he regarded women as mere sexual objects—an attitude that was not discouraged by his father—and used them without qualm. He does not feel that he and his father were in any sense competing with each other in a sexual arena, or that Howard was reliving his youth vicariously by promoting his son's sexual activities. He believes that his father did his best to encourage his son to share his tastes and interests, which happened to be sports and sex, and that he succeeded fully.

Jack's view of women changed drastically when he met his wife, Monique. She is the first "real woman" he has met, he says, the first woman with whom things did not begin and end in sex for him. He discovered other dimensions in her, aspects he did not find or even looked for in other women. Her appearance in his life "magically" put an end to Jack's womanizing, and he cannot even imagine ever being unfaithful to her. He has no logical or psychological explanation for the profound way Monique has affected him; he simply believes that she came into his life at a time when he was ready to take a "fresh look at women," and she just happened to be the perfect woman for him. He admits to having been surprised when his father approved of her immediately, because he had taken it for granted that Howard did not really want him to get married. He cannot cite any evidence to support why he felt that way, for Howard never actually said anything to him that could be construed as a discouragement of marriage. He just assumed that it was implicit in their relationship—two buddies all the way.

It has never occurred to Jack to compare his father's attitude toward women with his mother's toward men, and when the idea was proposed to him he seemed to be ill at ease. After some thought, he said that "things like that" were not comparable, and it was not even a matter of one being a man and the other a woman. From his perspective, his father was the sort of person for whom it was appropriate to behave the way he did, whereas his mother was not. It was in his nature, it was not in hers. That is why he admires him and rejects her.

Stephanie's perspective is very different from Jack's and Howard's. She has hardly any childhood memories of her father, and this, in her view, enables her to be much more objective about him than Jack is because she got to know him as a "person rather than as a father." She claims she is very glad that it happened that way as she cannot even imagine Howard being a good father to a daughter. She almost credits him for being aware of this himself and therefore not even trying.

As she recollects it, Howard's very rare visits to her mother's house had nothing to do with her and would have taken place at the same frequency if she had not existed. Their only purpose was "to hassle mother for sex," and they were sometimes successful, sometimes not. She thinks her mother is a sexy lady who does not have much else going for herself, and she has done the best she could with her life. Stephanie firmly believes that neither one of her parents should ever have had children or even gotten married.

It is not surprising to learn that Stephanie regarded herself unwanted as far back as she can remember. She claims to have arrived at that conclusion when she was about five and to have said to herself in effect, To hell with them, I'll look after myself from now on. She has always been quite self-sufficient and, like her brother, took an early and keen interest in sex; also like her brother, she learned a great deal at the maternal bedroom door. When she was thirteen, she installed a tape recorder under her mother's bed and sold the tape at school at the rate of ten dollars per half hour. She even had a couple of tapes of her father and mother together, and "really got off on them," she says now with a smile.

Stephanie thinks that her mother must have taken money

from some of her men at least, because they lived much better than Howard's support payments could have permitted. She was given private lessons in piano, French, and fencing, and at thirteen she seduced the fencing instructor—a man in his forties. She was already proficient in contraceptive techniques and familiar with sex literature, and by sixteen she has gone through all the positions described in the *Kama Sutra* with various lovers—all of them chosen by Stephanie. By her own account, her sex life has always been sleazy, and she places full blame on both her parents for her unsettled sexuality. She is not ambitious for a career but plans to become a songwriter because she has a lot to say about society. Her feelings toward her parents—especially her father—are admittedly bitter. She says he is a lecherous jock who never grew up—"He did not bring up his son, he cloned him." The only saving aspect of Jack's life, she feels, is his wife, Monique: if she stays with him, he may yet become his own man.

It is difficult not to agree with Stephanie's assessment of her father and brother. The former's interest in life certainly does not extend beyond sports and sex, even in his old age, and the latter has modeled himself on his father so completely that he is barely visible himself. Unlike Michael's descendants who idealized character traits and moral values, Jack adopted his father's style of behavior, an attitude toward life, without adding any hues and dimensions of his own. While his stable marriage might indicate a rejection of his father's way of life, it is totally unconscious, and Jack would never admit to it if it were proposed to him.

Howard worked hard at being a father, and by all the rules of "fathering" he was so good at it that his son idealized him as a child and continued to do so as a grown-up. He is being admired exactly for what he is, unendowed by qualities he does not actually possess; as far as his son's needs go, he is perfect, and no father could expect more from his son.

Howard did not work at all at being a father to his daughter, and her images of men are still confused at the age of twenty. The only language she has learned is that of sexuality, and she is already disappointed in its potential. She will need to learn other modes, other approaches to life if she is to overcome her self-perceived unwantedness.

It is clear that the interrelationships of Howard, Jack, and Stephanie were strongly influenced by the mother's overactive sexuality. Jack's idealization of his father was certainly reinforced by it, and it is tempting to say that Stephanie was seduced into imitating it.

Betty is in her late forties, a contented housewife in the twentieth year of her second marriage, mother of two daughters, Caroline, eighteen, and Joan, sixteen. Her father, Gregory, has been dead for twenty-five years and she lost touch with her mother many years ago. She is an uncommonly satisfied person and an exceedingly intelligent one; she turns wistful and pensive only when she talks about her father, but she likes to talk about him often and at length.

Betty is a European who did not come to the United States until her second marriage. Her father served in the consular corps of his country, and Betty spent her first eighteen years of life in four countries, all in Europe. Her mother was independent, both professionally and financially, and did not accompany her husband and only daughter on tours of duty. She joined them for Christmas and Easter, and they spent vacations with her either in their homeland or at a European spa.

Betty was brought up almost entirely by her father, who was in complete charge of her education. Like other embassy and consulate children in the Europe of the 1930s and 1940s, she was privately tutored and had very little contact with the people of the countries she lived in. She spent her days first with a nanny, and later with tutors, being taken on walks and studying hard, always waiting for daddy to come home from the office. When he did come home, he spent the remainder of the day with his daughter, checking on her homework, taking her to restaurants for dinner, and winding up the day by reading her to sleep when she was very young. When Betty was old enough to do her own reading, they would spend the evening in the drawing room, with Gregory immersed in his readings of philosophy—which was his main interest in life—and Betty doing homework or reading novels.

Betty loved their evenings together and she is glowingly nostalgic about them today. Gregory would often pause in his reading to discuss certain fine points of philosophy with her, and then she was encouraged to interrupt him with questions of her own, prompted by her reading. As she got older and her education progressed, they would sometimes get into elaborate discussions on such matters as the relationship of ethics and aesthetics, the problems of translating poetry, or the complexities in the libretto of *Don Giovanni*. Gregory did not try to dominate these discussions and allowed Betty free rein, but he always corrected her when she made an erroneous reference or an imprecise quote.

The onset of World War II found them stationed in Italy, and although Betty was only seven, international politics and the progress of the war became an important element in their discussions. Their country was neutral in the war, but Gregory was a passionate anti-Fascist in particular and anti-totalitarian in general, and he was pained at having to serve in a Fascist country. He inculcated Betty with his political beliefs, and today she is vehement on the subject of the Soviet Union and Latin American dictatorships.

Little mention was made of mother by either husband or daughter, but when they were together, there was no tension among them. She had a busy career as a trial lawyer, the only female one in her country, and she entertained them with stories from her practice. Gregory was quieter than usual when she was with them, but he seemed attentive and polite. Betty does recollect occasional pangs of resentment at her mother's absence and her inadequate interest in the lives of her husband and daughter, but she was always able to rid herself of such feelings by thinking of how good it was to live with father.

Betty's youth was entirely innocent of any knowledge of sex. The subject simply never came up, and if she did have any stirrings in adolescence, she certainly does not recall them now. She discovered sex on her first wedding night when she was twenty-one; her mother, who was present during the wedding preparations, made no attempt to enlighten her or even to find out if she needed to be enlightened. In retrospect, she thinks her father must have been asexual during the years of her growing up. She was close enough to him to have noticed if he had any contacts with women, but she has not, and she remembers very clearly that her parents slept in separate bedrooms whenever they spent time together. Years later, she found out inadvertently that her mother had had a long-standing affair with a prominent politician throughout the war years.

At every opportunity—and one seemed to arise every day—Gregory exhorted Betty to pursue a scholarly career and shun the temptations of business and domesticity. Only the life of the scholar is pure and sheltered from the disorders of the world, he would say, and all other human activity is tainted with particles of corruption. He often inveighed against his own choice of career, imposed on him by the urgings of his mother for reasons of security and prestige. His father's life as a village shopkeeper was a tenuous one economically and his mother persuaded Gregory that the only way for a boy of his class to advance in society was to distinguish himself in his studies and gain admittance to a branch of the civil service.

Gregory did distinguish himself, he told Betty, but regretted the use to which he put his success. Instead of following the scholarly path, he allowed himself to be seduced by the glitter of diplomatic service, and now he was trapped. It was his hope that his daughter, who was in a better position to make choices than he had been in, would make a wiser decision. He was never specific about his advice, he never pointed to a defined course she might follow; everything was couched in the general terms of ''scholarship'' and ''learning.''

During the last two years of the war, Gregory was transferred to a Central European country where air raids by Allied planes were an almost daily event. All other members of the legation sent their families to the safety of their homeland except Gregory. This was the subject of glowing pride for Betty then and now; it conferred special status on her both individually and socially. She felt especially loved and needed by her father, and she basked in the extra attention she was receiving from everyone as the only dependent at the legation. She remembers those two years as perhaps the happiest of her life, despite the frequent descents to the bomb shelter at all hours of the day and night.

Unlike countless others who remember time spent in bomb shelters with dread, Betty recalls it with special pleasure. During night raids, she would lie on a bench with her head in her father's lap and listen to the sounds of the antiaircraft guns and bombs falling sometimes dangerously close by. Occasionally, she would even fall asleep in the middle of a raid, and she was never afraid. During the day, her father would read to her during alerts, and it was all very cozy and romantic for a girl of twelve and thirteen. Betty is not ashamed to admit that when the war ended, she almost missed the air raids and the dim, dusty shelter.

Soon after the war, Gregory was posted to a newborn ''people's republic'' where his unhappiness with his work intensified. He detested having to deal with Communist functionaries even more than he had Fascists, who at least observed diplomatic etiquette. He saw to it that Betty's education was extended to political science and sociology, and his own philosophical studies centered on Burke, Hobbes, and John Stuart Mill. He became almost obsessed with such subjects as individual rights versus the state, democracy, and the class struggle. He told Betty that he was just then discovering the important role of class in his life, as well as in all societies. He was realizing that he had been ashamed of his humble origins, and that his choice of diplomacy as a career may have had a lot to do with that. He advised Betty not to share his preoccupation with class, not to use it as a criterion in making choices in her own life.

Betty's admiration for her father was intense, and she was amazed and hurt to discover that her feelings were not shared by her peers at the legations. They said he was a bookworm and a snob who thought he was too good to mingle with others—a notion that had never occurred to Betty. She had vehement arguments on the subject, fiercely defending her father, unwaveringly loyal. She also found out during these exchanges that others felt quite differently about their fathers than she did. They resented having to live in a foreign country and blamed their fathers for it. They felt neglected and isolated; some drank secretly and others hinted at unnamed vices.

When Betty was nineteen, Gregory was promoted and transferred back home, which came as a shock for both. They were so accustomed to living with each other that readjustment to a household that included mother was rather traumatic for Betty, and appeared to be no less so for Gregory. As for mother, she was seemingly indifferent and went about her business without taking even a day off when they arrived. The relationship between Gregory and his wife continued to be polite and correct, but totally lacking in displayed affection. Betty was equally civil to her mother and received mannerly treatment from her, but their dealings were also devoid of exchanges of even the merest affection.

Betty entered the university and her schedule often did not match her father's; the two could no longer luxuriate in spending a great deal of time together. Still, she never went to bed without dropping in on her father in his study to discuss the events of the day and whatever intellectual problems they were grappling with. He continued to praise the virtues of scholarship and the advantages of the scholarly life, without specifically pressing Betty in a particular direction. He accepted her choice of medieval history as her subject without any argument in behalf of his beloved philosophy, and showed great interest in her studies. He encouraged her to develop an active social life and admitted feeling somewhat guilty for having deprived her of it during her childhood and teens. The only subject he never brought up was his wife; the only subject she never brought up was her mother.

Socially, the move back home was overwhelming for Betty. From the splendid isolation of consulates and embassies where father was always available, where the two of them formed and shaped their own world, where everything was safe and defined, she found herself transposed to the swirl of the real world. The vastness of the university, the multitude of people she had to cope with each day, the reduced presence of her father, her laconic mother, all these new realities pressed down on her and she was not prepared for them in any way. She reacted by holding herself back from all but the necessary contacts, by responding minimally. She surrounded herself with study, as if to insulate herself from intrusions, leaving space only for her father.

Betty was receiving a great deal of attention from men, mostly at the university, and she responded coolly and politely. Coolly, because that was her way of standing back and waiting; politely, because she was inculcated by her father with the importance of politeness. "Politeness is an important means of defending civilization," he would say, and it was a matter of principle for both to be unvaryingly, passionately polite. A young instructor became especially interested in her, impressed by her command of languages, and they had long discussions on the historical meanings of gallantry and chivalry. They spent considerable time together, sipping tea, or walking to the library, but Betty thought of him only as a faculty member, a figure of authority, an elder.

She remained entirely innocent of sex and had no close women friends who might have pressed the point with her throughout her university years. It seems incredible to her today that she had gone through adolescence and young adulthood without any expression of sexuality, even in dreams. She was also unaware of any sexual activity around her, either at home or among her classmates, although she knows that there was a lot of promiscuity on campus. At home, her parents continued to maintain separate bedrooms and the atmosphere remained untroubled by passions of any sort.

Betty received her doctorate when she was twenty-three and was about to accept an appointment to the faculty when her father was killed in an airplane crash. She remembers her first reaction as having been "a great, silent scream," followed by a long period of "interior emptiness." She has absolutely no recollection of the funeral, although she knows she attended it, and recalls nothing about her mother during that period, as if she did not exist. She does remember the comforting presence of the young instructor, Kurt, in a general sense but without details. An entire year following Gregory's death has been erased from Betty's memory. She knows that she continued to live at home, she knows that she did not accept her appointment at the university, but she cannot document any given event during that period.

Her first memory is that of Kurt's asking her to marry him. Her first reaction was a feeling of distance, as if they had been enveloped in thick fog, and she distinctly recalls slowly emerging from it, day by day, hour by hour. She did not think she loved Kurt, certainly not the way she loved her father, and she had no other points of reference. Her mother, whose longtime lover was now a frequent visitor at their house, urged her to accept on the grounds that Kurt came from an excellent family with old money and good connections, but Betty hesitated; her father's death had purged her of all feeling, and she was coping with life only through instincts and intellect. She wavered for a month, trying to imagine what her father would have thought of Kurt and of her marrying him, and at the end she said yes, because it was polite. They had a large wedding and toured Europe on their honeymoon. At Betty's request, their first stops were the cities where she had lived with her father as a child and teenager, and it was in one of these cities that their marriage was consummated.

Betty seems to be still startled at the effect her sexual initiation had on her life. She had expected to feel nothing, but found herself so overwhelmed by passion that she lost control of her senses. She says today that it was exactly like a defloration scene in a pornographic novel, where the originally reticent heroine turns into a ferociously lustful female. She was totally astonished, but, contrary to what she had thought was her nature, she was able to put her astonishment aside without intellectual analysis and abandon herself to her feelings.

Betty's amazement was exceeded only by Kurt's, although he was too polite to mention it during the first year of their marriage, which was spent in a sea of passion, with little time devoted to anything else. Kurt was an experienced lover who took delight in teaching her lust's ways of expression, and if he was concerned about neglecting his career, he said nothing about it to Betty. Meanwhile, she gave up all thoughts of her own career and could hardly bring herself ever to leave the house. She did not maintain contact with her mother, and, lacking friends, her life revolved entirely around Kurt. She thought less about her father during that year than in any other period of her life, though she does remember wondering what he would have said about her sexual discoveries.

There was little exchange between Betty and Kurt during the first year aside from sex, which was a complete reversal of their former relationship. As the blaze of their passions began to dampen, they had to get virtually reacquainted intellectually and become acquainted in other ways. Betty had known very little about Kurt, except for his mind, and now that she was beginning to know him, not everything she learned pleased her. Kurt's status as an authority figure dissolved during their first year, and Betty was now looking at him with a different slant; passion had made them equals, and Betty's new perspective revealed aspects of Kurt previously unseen.

What became evident first of all was that Kurt was not the pure, idealistic intellectual she had imagined him to be. It emerged that he had chosen Romance languages and literature as his field because he had known French and Italian since childhood, which enabled him to master the subject with substantially less effort. It also emerged that he was keenly ambitious in his career and planned his path to the chairmanship of the department in minute detail. His lack of interest in having children stemmed from his career plans, which included attaining international fame, not by means of scholarly work but through organizing symposia and founding journals in his field, financed with his family's money. Betty had assumed that his opposition to children, like her own, was philosophically based, and she was gravely disturbed by what she discovered.

She started to think about her father again, often. Compared to his idealism and devotion to scholarship, Kurt's worldly concerns and impure motives seemed shallow, almost contemptible, and while she and Kurt still had many common interests, she was beginning to get suspicious about all his intellectual claims. The second year of their marriage was marked by her rapidly sinking respect for Kurt and her developing sense of guilt toward her father for having betrayed him; if Kurt's intellectual pretenses were sham, as they increasingly seemed to be, then her marriage to him was indeed a betrayal of Gregory.

She confronted Kurt with her changing views of him, but he fended them off by saying that Betty was out of touch with the world, indeed was never in touch with it. As for Gregory's scholarly views, it was easy for him to hold them because he was an amateur and could well afford to be pure from the lofty, elegant perspective of embassies and consulates. Betty could not tolerate attacks on her father and retaliated by constructing elaborate sexual fantasies during her lovemaking with Kurt, something she had never indulged in before. At first, she fantasized about movie stars and other public figures having sex with her instead of Kurt, and in fact by this time it was the only way she could maintain passionate interest. As the effectiveness of this method faded, she began substituting images of men she actually knew and found attractive, which was much more satisfactory both sexually and as a means of retaliation.

Then, one night, instead of the conjured-up image of an acquaintance, there appeared the uninvoked presence of her father making love to her. After a few moments of unendurable ecstasy, Betty fainted, and when she came to she found herself in a hospital bed. Kurt had been so frightened by her passing out that he summoned an ambulance; as it happened, she did not respond to efforts to resuscitate her for a considerable time. She felt stunned, as if she had taken a large dose of sleeping pills after climbing a mountain. She ached everywhere, there was a ringing in her ears, she was dizzy.

She was kept in the hospital for several days, but nothing was found. Her symptoms had lifted by the time she was released, although she still felt emotionally stunned and physically drained. Kurt was sympathetic and supportive, but she felt unable to feel grateful and told him nothing about her experience. She stayed in bed for several weeks, feeling nothing, refusing to communicate with Kurt, tormented by dreams about her father. Every night he would appear, always bearing a weapon of some sort, menacing Betty with a stiletto or a Sten gun or a brick in his hand. He would come very close to stabbing or shooting her; just as the blade plunged toward her, when his finger tightened on the trigger, she would awaken with a start.

She was certain that her father's appearance in her bed and the subsequent dreams were manifestations of her festering guilt feelings about marrying Kurt, and she had no other choice but to leave him. He was uncomprehending and astonished when she told him her decision, but she refused to offer him any reasons. He tried to persuade her that she was having a nervous breakdown and should allow herself to be treated, but to no avail. She was convinced that she was paying the price for having betrayed her father's standards and expectations, and it could not be avoided or substituted for. She instructed her lawyer to begin divorce proceedings, took the money her father had left her in life insurance, and bought an airplane ticket to New York. It was very far away, there was an ocean to cross, and it seemed to be the place to go.

The next two years of Betty's life were a time of physical floundering and mental stock-taking. She was only twenty-six, educated and attractive, and she set out to think things through while she drifted across America. She took temporary jobs here and there, sometimes as a typist, sometimes as a translator, and for the first time in her life she began to mingle with people. She found Americans to be easier than others to talk to, and she was able to form casual but friendly relationships at her workplaces. She avoided sexual involvements, but got to know more men than she ever had. She realized how narrow her life had been, despite having lived in so many countries and having been married and divorced. She thought a lot about happiness which she had known only while she lived with her father, dismissing the first year of her marriage as a result of liberated repression. Perhaps, she noted in the journal she kept, she was one of that breed of men and women who cannot be made happy. "Happiness eludes them as music eludes the tone deaf. They are solitary, they are sad, they are beyond consolation. They act as if they had once arrived too late to the ultimate, the divine rendezvous, and nothing could possibly console them for what they had missed."

Another time, she wrote, "Unhappiness is solitude, tedium, probing curiosity, perplexing passions, men passing through, homelessness. In a word, unlike happiness, it is a *genre*. Happiness, on the other hand, is not a feeling, nor is it an attitude toward life. It is a certain fullness, a certain serious, concentrated, almost grave, focusing on life." Betty was realizing that her father was the only person in her life on whom she had focused in a concentrated, serious way and wondered if it would be possible for her to recapture the intensity of feelings between them and transpose it into a love relationship.

By this time, Betty was very well read in psychoanalytic literature and was intelligent enough to perceive the nature of the bond between her and Gregory, but after contemplating about it for some time she decided against seeking psychotherapeutic help. She thought it was the easy way out, if it was a way out at all, and not suited for intellectuals. Besides, she worked as translator at an international psychoanalytic conference for a week, and the members of the profession she met there did not inspire much confidence in her. She felt very strongly that she had to work out her life by herself.

Betty had been wandering through America for two years, probing and thinking, when she took a temporary job in a brokerage house. One day, she met the owner of the business in the elevator, and he turned out to be a compatriot of hers who had immigrated to America with his parents when he was five. They had lunch, then dinner, then breakfast, and one day Betty felt and knew with absolute certainty that she was in love for the first time. Mel was ten years older than she, divorced, and very knowledgeable on a wide range of subjects; he was also attentive and patient. Her feelings for him had the intensity of closeness she had experienced with her father, as well as the intensity of passion she had with Kurt, and the two blended harmoniously. Betty learned the truth of E. M. Forster's observation that "the affections are more reticent than the passions."

They have been happily married for twenty years now, and Betty has been quite content to be wife and mother and not enter academic life. Mel was a more than adequate intellectual partner, and she did not feel deprived of mental stimulation at any time. She brought up Caroline and Joan in the spirit of her father, in the sense that she emphasized the life of the mind as the most worthy pursuit to be engaged in, and Mel agreed with her completely on the subject. The girls are obviously very bright and well adjusted; Caroline is about to enter college and plans to become an economist, and Joan, only sixteen, is wavering between art history and architecture. One could not expect to meet a happier family.

Betty's idealization of her father was extraordinary and indomitable, even if we consider the hothouse atmosphere of her childhood and adolescence. He did seem to be an admirable person indeed, unlike Howard, and he brought up his daughter affectionately and purposefully. He was not authoritarian or repressive, yet managed to imbue Betty with a dedication to intellectual pursuits, individual liberty, and moral integrity. Although she was derailed twice by emotional factors from following her chosen profession, she has never denounced the primacy of the life of the mind, and appears to have passed the torch to her own daughters with a good likelihood of success.

If Betty's self-image is rooted in her idealization of Gregory, so is her sexuality. There is no reason to think that he was seductive or sexually suggestive, or that he was repressive and inhibiting in that respect. Their isolation, coupled with the total absence of information about sex, apparently produced a self-generated repression in Betty that was absolute for the first twenty-three years of her life, and when the lid was finally lifted, her sexuality emerged explosively. After burning off its long built-up pressures, it revealed its primary, original object when her father appeared uninvoked in her sexual fantasies. Her subsequent guilt was seemingly purged during her wanderings, aided by her keen self-perception and, one suspects, a good deal of luck, for her life could have turned out tragically without it.

macho, competitive

Kenneth is in his late forties, a diminutive man with a stern expression, entirely lacking any sense of humor. He is internationally known as a chef de cuisine, and at the present time he presides over the kitchen of a restaurant in a southern city. He has worked in top restaurants in New York, Chicago, and Los Angeles; he is a restless man and an irritable one who is apt to pack up his knives and quit a job at a slight insult. As one of the few American chefs of major reputation, he commands top pay and does not have to be concerned about not getting job offers from the best places. He has been married for twenty-seven years, having met his wife, Dolores, in a hotel kitchen where he was serving as apprentice cook and she as cashier. They have two sons, Neil, twenty-five, and Donald, twenty-two.

Kenneth grew up in the Northwest and still has a fondness for that region. He talks at length about riding his pony in the forest and about the taste of trout caught fifteen minutes before it is eaten; he used to take the boys there on his summer vacations, but now that they are grown, his visits are less frequent. He was brought up by his mother and grandmother, who owned a rustic hotel known for its home cooking, and as they worked long hours, Kenneth was left relatively free to roam around. The hotel was built by his father, a contractor, who abandoned his family soon after Kenneth was born, never to be seen or heard from again.

When Kenneth was little, his mother would keep him in the hotel kitchen so as to keep an eye on him, and he came to be interested in food and cooking early on. He was helping out by the time he was six and preparing breakfasts soon after. He liked to experiment with foods, and his first creation, a trout mousse, made its way into cookbooks while Kenneth was in his teens.

He was subjected to a lot of teasing and abuse by his peers, who regarded his interest in cooking as "sissy stuff," and he made special efforts to prove his mettle by participating in activities that did not really amuse him. In high school, he was a member of a "gang" modeled after movie gangsters; their purpose was to steal merchandise from stores and valuables from their own homes, sell or pawn them, and buy war surplus weapons with the proceeds. They used an abandoned hut in the woods for their warehouse and meetingplace, and it was soon bulging with goods. Kenneth found these games distasteful and he was always afraid of being caught, but in time the gang lost interest and the warehouse was soon overgrown by weeds, hiding its secret treasures.

Kenneth was always smaller than his peers and could not defend himself when they chose to beat him up, but he soon learned that if he went along with everything, or better yet, if he instigated illicit activities, the beatings would cease. He interpreted this to mean that if one excelled in something, such as instigation, one's reward would be immunity from harm, and he vowed that he would become the best in an as yet unchosen area of his life.

Another and more important cause of Kenneth's vulnerability was the fact that he alone in all the school had no father. He was teased and tormented mercilessly on that theme and suffered in silence when his mother was referred to in demeaning terms. His feelings about her were ambivalent; he would have liked to fight for her honor when she was called names, yet at the same time he resented that she could not hold on to his father, that she let him go. He never blamed him for leaving; it seemed quite natural that men should be able to come and go as they wished, but it was the duty of women to keep them. A "good woman" would never let her man go, and he was going to make sure that the woman he married would not.

These two notions—excellence and the need for a good woman—implanted themselves in Kenneth's consciousness early in his life. By age thirteen, he decided on his life's work and from then on he spent practically all his time in the hotel kitchen, memorizing all the recipes in *Escoffier* and experimenting with dishes of his own design. He did not even date in high school, mainly because girls were not interested in the smallest boy in the class who cooked for fun, but he always knew that a good woman would come along sooner or later. After high school, he persuaded his mother to send him to Switzerland to sharpen his culinary skills; he apprenticed with one of the masters of the profession, and in his third year there he met and soon married his wife, Dolores.

As Kenneth recalls it, he was feeling very cocky at twenty-one, what with a new wife and three years of apprenticeship with the best to his credit, and he decided that nothing less than opening his own restaurant would do. He chose a city on the West Coast where the competition in haute cuisine was minimal, and with money borrowed from his mother he opened a rather large restaurant. It was Dolores's job to run the dining room and Kenneth's to market and work the kitchen, and it soon became apparent that their combined inexperience was running the operation into the ground. Although the venture could have been salvaged by hiring a competent manager, Kenneth petulantly decided to abandon ship and bail out, leaving his mother with a considerable financial loss. He declared that he was an artist who should not be bothered with commercial considerations, and from now on he would devote himself only to creating meals; as for his mother, she had just inherited some money from her mother and could well afford it. This was the first of his many sudden moves from kitchen to kitchen, but he never tried to open a restaurant again. Nor did Dolores ever leave home and hearth after their joint failure.

Neil was born soon after, and Kenneth was determined from the start that he was going to make the boy the second greatest chef in the country. He could not expect Neil to have more talent for cooking than he had, but even if he did, it was not permissible for a son to surpass his father. Also, he was going to see to it that the boy not become a sissy but learn to defend himself before he entered first grade. In Kenneth's view, Neil had every reason to be proud of his father from the moment he was born, and he was going to make sure that he had every reason to be proud of his son. Dolores was "an obedient wife and a natural mother," and could be completely trusted to do his bidding. He claims he knew "instinctively" that he was going to be a great father because he remembered all too clearly how it felt not to have one and knew exactly what "services" a father is expected to provide to his son.

Kenneth seems to remember everything about Neil's childhood; he can put a date on the day he took his first steps or spoke his first words or put on his little chef's hat. Neil's first toys were cooking utensils, and his playpen was littered with miniature pots and pans. He was given his first French lesson at four, because Kenneth knew how important French was in the world of cooking; he himself wasted considerable time in Switzerland learning it before he could really understand what was happening in the kitchen. At five, Neil was taking karate lessons to prepare him for the vicissitudes of school.

Real cooking lessons began at six, just after school, because Kenneth had to return to work in midafternoon. Neil took to it very well, as Kenneth recalls it, having a natural dexterity that Kenneth himself had to learn through a lot of practice. The boy could turn out a passable meal, from soup to nuts, by the time he was nine, at which time it became his job to cook dinner for his mother, his younger brother, who was born three years after he was, and himself. According to Kenneth, Dolores, "like all women," was just an average cook, and making dinner on a regular basis was going to provide Neil with both practice and the acceptance of daily routine.

Kenneth paused briefly at this point to acknowledge the existence of his second son, Donald. His birth was something of a shock for Kenneth, who was certain that it was going to be a girl; he had planned to bring her up to be a "perfect wife and mother, because we certainly need them in this world." Having another son put him at a temporary loss; for the first couple of years, he did not know what to do with him.

To return to Neil, he was doing quite well at school, and nobody dared to tease him about cooking because of his prowess at karate and jiujitsu. He continued to enjoy cooking as a routine, and Kenneth insisted that he participate in as many school sports as he could find time for. He was popular with his schoolmates, both boys and girls, and at thirteen he was two inches taller than his father. The only trouble was that he did not seem to show any signs of being an innovative cook; he could reproduce any recipe, no matter how complex, perfectly well, but was adding no individual flair to it, no inspiration.

Kenneth decided that perhaps placing him in the working environment of an actual restaurant kitchen might ignite his dormant talents, and he arranged for a colleague to take him on as an apprentice, working dinners only, so as not to interfere with other required activities. He recalls proudly how hard Neil was working in those days. He was up by six to do his homework, in school till three, occupied with sports for a couple of hours, off to the restaurant by six, home after eleven. Kenneth made it a point to go to football or basketball practice each day with the special permission of the coaches to see Neil and cheer him on, and on weekends he would take him to various sports events, depending on what sport was in season.

Meanwhile, Kenneth had decided that the future for Donald lay in the hotel industry, and he instructed the boy to make sure to get top grades to aid his admission to one of the leading hotel administration schools. He also urged him to become acquainted with the general topic of hotels; he helped him to build a substantial collection of brochures from hotels all over the world, indexed country by country, and gave him surprise quizzes from time to time. When he was fifteen, Donald could recite the room rates and other important details of any hotel that accommodated tourists anywhere in the world. On Sundays, when Kenneth and Dolores often had friends over, Donald would be presented as a production number. Someone would say, "Grand Hotel, Nürnberg," and he would reel off the various room rates, the number of rooms available, the features of the menu in the main dining room, and the banquet facilities.

After a year's apprenticeship, it was clear to Kenneth that Neil was not going to become the second greatest chef in America, and it now became a question of what to do about him. Could he live with the knowledge that his first son was just an ordinary chef, after all those years of preparation? It did not take him long to realize that he could not, and with great reluctance he decided to pull him out of his job and put him in the restaurant supply business. He put up the capital and made the initial contacts, taking 25 percent of the gross profits for himself for the time being. He regretted only that it was too late to turn Donald into a chef, for he was well launched toward a hotel career, having been admitted to the school of Kenneth's choice.

Neil was now twenty-five and doing well in business. On the whole, Kenneth is not unhappy about him, nor does he glow with pride. He is looking forward to the day when Neil finds himself a wife and has a few kids of his own, and also expects that he will build the business into a national operation. They get together every Sunday, and Neil is often asked to cook dinner for them and their friends.

Donald, on the other hand, has become a source of bitter disappointment to Kenneth, and he is hard put to even talk about him. The boy dropped out of hotel school after the first year and headed for New York to become an actor. He wrote his parents, but did not come home; contact with him has been tenuous ever since, though he suspects that Dolores may be in touch with him behind Kenneth's back.

Neil is a very handsome, athletic-looking young man, dressed according to the latest fashions. He talks easily and seems to be making a deliberate effort to appear charming; still, when it comes to talking about his father and about growing up, there is a hesitant look in his eyes and he speaks noticeably slower. He looks up to his father, he says, and is "just like him." He does not take women seriously, but expects to marry someday, not soon, in order to have children. He wants three at least, two boys and a girl, and he is already planning their careers. One of the boys will take over the business, which he expects to be "very big" by then, and the other will be in Wall Street; the girl should be a movie actress, a superstar.

He remembers his childhood as very happy, and he was more aware of his father than he was of his mother; all his toys seem to have come from him, and it was he who taught him "things." He became interested in cooking very early and really enjoyed puttering around with dishes. It never occurred to him for a moment that he was doing anything unusual until he got to school, and then he squelched the teasing with muscle. He always felt that cooking was a very masculine thing to do; it filled him with a sense of power to produce a meal and then watch people eating it. He does not remember a time when he did not think that his father was the greatest cook in the world; he had been to France twice and his trips confirmed his belief.

He never expected to equal his father's skills, but he did want to be one of the best and thinks he probably was. When Kenneth pulled him out of the restaurant, he was perplexed, even a bit hurt for a while, but eventually came to accept the decision. In the first place, he would never dream of opposing any decision of his father's, and he also believes that if you cannot be the best at something, you should find something else to do; for the same reason, he does not like team sports, only one-on-one confrontations. He expects to bring up his children by the same principles he and his father believe in and does not find rebelliousness acceptable. He thinks his brother is a "jerk" who has never taken anything seriously and that "he is afraid to show his face around here."

Neil did not have time for girls when he was an adolescent and he does not think they are very important in a man's life. He does not have relationships that last longer than a weekend or so, and does not even think about women when he is not with them. He likes "quickies" best and patronizes prostitutes frequently.

Donald is a very pleasant young man, the only one of his family with a sense of humor. He has no desire to see his father these days, but hopes that one day they will be able to sit down and have a "long talk about things." He is very happy being an actor and has no doubts about making it in the profession; he feels he was born for it, even though he did not discover his calling until he was in hotel school. He has nothing against the hotel business and was, in fact, mentally prepared to be in it. He likes the theatrical quality of hotels and thinks that everything within a hotel is "game-like, a make-believe"; going into a hotel is like going to a show where the guests constitute the audience.

Donald recalls his childhood as being "amusing." His father was not an active participant until he was in first grade, but Donald was quite happy with his mother's company. He has hardly any recollections of his brother during the early years, and even during school years Neil was away from home so much of the time that he does not really have a sense of knowing him. He is quick to point out, though, that his father and brother are exactly alike, and he is not convinced that Neil's imposed change of career resulted from his lack of first-rate talent for cooking. He suspects that he may have been first rate and was pulled out of the kitchen precisely because his father could not have tolerated being surpassed by a son.

When Donald was six, his father began talking to him about foreign countries, bribing him with a gift of a stamp collection. The bribe worked and the boy became keenly interested in geography, memorizing the capital cities of every country in the world and spending a great deal of time poring over atlases and stamps. After his basic interest was well established, Kenneth started to focus on the subject of hotels, which fascinated Donald immediately. He claims that sending away for brochures was his idea, as was the system of cataloguing them alphabetically, country by country. He distinctly remembers that his father acted surprised when he suggested it, as if a boy of eight had no capacity to generate ideas, and while he went along with it, he did not praise Donald.

As a direct result of that incident, Donald began to get suspicious of his father. He felt grateful to him for having aroused his interest in foreign lands and hotels, yet he felt stifled by his father's constant supervision of his activities. Why was this man constantly peering over his shoulder, always telling him what to do? He grew to detest the Sunday afternoon performances that were expected of him, although he still enjoyed learning about hotels. At the same time, unbeknown to his father, he became equally interested in literature, especially drama, and spent much of his time reading Shakespeare, Chekhov, Strindberg, and Pirandello—his favorites—while his father was at work.

Girls have always thought that he was "cute," and he liked them a lot, but the rules that governed his home life were such that it was difficult to find time for them. Most of the time, he resorted to lying about extracurricular activities, when in fact he was dating girls. He could not help but wonder about his brother's secret life, if he had one. Did he also see girls on the sly, or did he not date at all? He was reluctant to ask him, and the subject did not come up until Neil's senior prom, when he came home surprisingly early. The boys were alone in the house, and Donald summoned up the courage to ask Neil if he went out with girls. Neil was curt on the subject; women were nothing, really, he said. You get into their skirts, but there is not that much fun in that. If he ever got married, it would be mainly for the sake of having children and to be able to get in a quickie after coming home from work without having to worry about VD. He asked Donald if he liked girls and seemed puzzled when Donald said he liked them a lot, indeed.

Taking advantage of the opportunity, Donald tried to extend the conversation to other areas and asked Neil if he found father too intrusive. Neil seemed appalled at the question; he said that fathers were supposed to concern themselves with their children's activities and he would do the same if he were a father. Besides, he would probably never do anything if father did not keep after him. He did not appear to be eager to discuss things any further, and the two boys have not really had a close talk ever since.

By the time Donald left for hotel school, his view of his father was quite different from what it had been. He saw Kenneth as a vain, selfish person who wanted everything to go his way and everyone to do his bidding; he was insensitive and treated women as inferior creatures. Donald was still interested in the hotel business, but his interest was now totally divorced from his relationship with his father and he felt that he did not owe Kenneth anything. If he was going to succeed, his success was not going to be a prize to be presented to his father but an accomplishment for its own sake, to be cherished by himself; if he was going to fail, there would be no guilt, only regret over his lack of ability.

School was moderately interesting, but it did not engage Donald sufficiently. His readings in drama intensified, and at the urging of his girlfriend he joined a theater group where he was an immediate success. The stage provided the context he had been looking for in hotel life, where preparation and performance are everything; on the stage, Donald found that preparation and performance are but parts of something much larger and infinitely more exciting. He felt he had come home.

At the present time, Donald has no feelings at all about his father, as if he were a part of the past; he had his role and he played it. He does not exclude the possibility of a new role coming up sometime in the future, but meanwhile Kenneth is not a part of his life. At the end of our talks, Donald struck a dramatic pose and recited Gloucester's famous lines from *King Lear*:

Love cools,
Friendship falls off, brothers divide.
In cities, mutinies;
In countries, discord;
In palaces, treason,
and the bond crack'd
betwixt son and father. . . .

"Macho" and "competitive" are not thought of as twin traits, yet they appear together with surprising frequency. Kenneth is certainly both and we can see why. Growing up without a father is always extraordinarily difficult, and when the cause of fatherlessness is abandonment, the burden placed on the growing child can be intolerable, leading to all sorts of severe character disorders. Kenneth's way of lightening his burden was to shift blame away from his father and place it on his mother, thereby establishing the breeding ground of his machismo: the "good woman" is one who can hold on to her man. While Kenneth remained with his wife after their children were born, he did in effect reenact his father's departure by means of frequent changes of job, requiring moves to different destinations. Symbolically, he fulfilled the wish of every child to be like his father.

Kenneth's competitive nature is in part a product of his small stature and in part of his affinity for cooking—he had to compensate for the former and defend the latter, and the common denominator was excellence. Machismo and competitiveness worked well for Kenneth, enabling him to survive without severe psychological damage and, most importantly, to succeed. He even succeeded in passing on those traits to his older son, and his inner need to pass them on, to mould his children to his own specifications, was clearly compelling for Kenneth. His failure to affect Donald is a great blow to him—once abandoned by father, now abandoned by son.

The wounds of childhood never heal entirely, and his life-long hostility toward women is a salve. For Neil, on the other hand, it is an attitude that has no apparent cause other than paternal influence; he took it over, inherited it intact, as he had most of his father's attitudes and beliefs. Unlike children who have idealized their fathers, Neil does not give Kenneth credit; for him, it is a given that the son should be like the father, and it follows that Donald must be a deviant.

One might say that the only irrevocable event in life is the moment when one decides whether to remain in the family, the class, the tradition, or to go one's way and become rootless and free. Neil and Donald illustrate these choices, and each has made the decision that is appropriate to himself, although it is too soon to know whether their decisions will be successful.

Joe has just turned sixty and is very conscious of it. He would not admit to being vain, which is not one of the manly virtues, but he quite natty in dress, with neatly trimmed hair and mustache. He has recently retired from the army after forty years of service as a noncommissioned officer and he is restless. He does not quite know what to do with himself; after he does exercises for an hour—a lifetime habit—he plays some baseball with kids on the playground, goes for a long walk, takes a swim, and spends the rest of the time watching television. He assiduously avoids the company of other retired people living in the seaside town because "they think old," and he talks only with the kids on the playground. He is thinking of putting his savings into buying a dry-cleaning store or an automotive supply business and he carefully scouts locations on his walks.

Joe grew up in the Midwest, the only son of an auto mechanic who owned his own garage. His mother was an invalid who spent most of her time in bed and could pay little attention to her son or husband, and Joe practically lived in the garage where his father could keep an eye on him. He was a good boy, he said, "by nature," who gave his parents little trouble. He was intensely interested in anything mechanical and taught himself to take apart and put together again almost any device. He cannot recall ever having any store-bought toys or ever wanting any, and he was perfectly satisfied to putter about with flashlights, old clocks, or discarded automobile parts.

Joe's father was the strong, silent type who did not like to repeat himself and was quick with a backhand slap. He was a "steady drinker," taking nips all day long and spending his evenings in a saloon, but Joe does not remember ever seeing him drunk. When he came home late at night, he was not unruly; he tiptoed into the bedroom where his parents slept in separate beds, and the little boy could sometimes hear them talk in a low voice. No voice was ever raised in the house, but Joe was aware of a certain tension between his parents, a state he could not identify. Today, he thinks it must have been a sex problem, because his mother was unavailable sexually and also unable to engage in it.

Joe became knowledgeable about sex early on. Often, he noticed various women coming to the garage during lunch hour and after closing time, and they would stay in the back office with his father for a considerable time. He was never told not to come into the office, and one day he walked in to find his father lying on the floor, with a woman sitting astride him, both apparently fully clothed. She screamed at him to get out, and Joe never again tried to go into the office when a woman was visiting. He expected to be punished, but his father said nothing about the incident then or later, which really aroused Joe's curiosity. He learned all he could about sex from older boys, one of whom taught him to masturbate when he was seven.

He was not very good at school, because he was more interested in manual activities than in mental exercises. His attention wandered most of the time, and the motivation to learn to read came mainly from his desire to read technical instructions. By the time he was ten, he had his own work-shop in a corner of the garage, and there was hardly any-thing he could not fix. He worked part time for his father and used the money he made for buying his own tools, and although he liked girls, he preferred to spend his time in his shop with a couple of special friends. He planned on becom-ing an engineer, but when he broached the subject to his fa-ther, he was curtly told that engineers did what they were told and "they had to kiss ass." It was much better to be a mechanic, because you had to concern yourself only with the machine; you fixed what was wrong and did not have to worry about your boss. This was one of only two times Joe could recall when he received what could be construed as advice from his father.

Joe freely admits that he "went a bit wild" as a teenager. Every once in a while, he and his cronies would steal a car and take it for a "test ride," purely out of mechanical curi-osity, but they always returned it intact and never got caught. He also had a liking for "wild girls" who did not waste his time, and brags about having spent a lot of time in backseats with a girl and a bottle. He recalls those days fondly and hates the idea of being sixty years old. He started drinking as a teenager, always rum or gin, but he could hold his liquor just as well as his father. His mother died when he was eighteen; soon after, he got a girl pregnant and ran away to join the army on his father's advice.

The army agreed with him immediately. He liked every-thing about it; it was a place where a man could make friends and know exactly where he stood. Everything was clearly defined and everything had its proper place; if a man made a mistake, he had only himself to blame. What Joe liked best of all was that one could make his way up and ac-quire authority over others. Authority was appealing and precise—one did not have to live in doubt, as in civilian life, because the answers were all there to all the questions one could possibly have.

World War II came soon after Joe joined the army, and he was one of the first to be in combat in the Pacific. Combat, too, was very agreeable to Joe, because it was simple and clear-cut; you took an order and executed it, you killed to avoid getting killed. It was exciting to be in constant danger, even the noise was stimulating. He hated to see some of his friends get killed, and when it happened it spurred him on to get revenge. He was fearless but not reckless and soon became widely known for his valor; within the first year, he made sergeant and won a chestful of medals.

He came through the war without a scratch and with an excellent reputation for handling men in and out of combat. He had turned down several opportunities for battlefield commissions because he wanted to stay close to his men. As a sergeant, he could give an order and see it carried out immediately; as an officer, he would have to rely on his noncoms. He wanted to be in the thick of the action with a weapon in his hand, not behind it talking into a field phone.

When the war was over, he considered returning to civilian life as a mechanic, perhaps with a small lot for used cars, but soon dismissed the notion and reenlisted. He was stationed in the Southwest and had an easy life in the sun, so he decided to get married; his father, who had never answered his letters during the war, had died recently, and Joe was all alone in the world. There were plenty of women available and Joe picked Rose, "a frail thing, who didn't look like she'd give a man any trouble." Nine months later, she gave birth to Keith, and at two-year intervals to Nancy and Janet, and died in childbirth with the last.

It was difficult to bring up small children on an army base, and Joe got married again, mainly to have a mother for the children. Unfortunately, he did not choose well, for it turned out that his second wife did not really like children, and Joe got married still another time when the oldest child was seven. That marriage lasted three years or so, after which she left him for another man. At that point, Joe decided not to get married again; he figured that Keith was now old enough to look after the girls.

Joe claims he was a good father—strict but affectionate. He set up a timetable for each child, which they had to follow or be ready to be punished. There was also a long-term timetable that determined that Keith was to become an engineer, and the girls would be married by the time they were twenty-one. Although Joe was transferred three or four times while the children were growing up, the children were instructed to pretend that they were always in the same place and to follow the same routine.

According to Joe, he had little trouble with them, yet his plans did not quite work out. Keith dropped out of high school without his father's permission and left home to become a country singer; he came to visit a couple of times, but Joe has not seen him for some ten years now. He assumes that Keith is on the road with his band and has "just plain lost touch," but he is a good boy and Joe is not worried about him. Nancy got married ahead of schedule at seventeen to a first lieutenant, in a kind of shotgun wedding—Joe chuckles as he recollects it. They were divorced after the baby was born, and a couple of years later, Nancy married another officer. She had a couple of more kids and they live on base in the South; he visited them one Christmas and they seemed OK, and he gets a postcard every once in a while. Janet did not meet the marital deadline at all and is still unmarried at thirty. She does not seem to be able to settle down and roams around from job to job. Unlike the other two, she visits Joe faithfully at unpredictable intervals, without announcing herself.

On the whole, Joe is not happy at the way his children have turned out and tends to blame it on the death of their mother and his "unlucky" marriages, yet he feels he did the best he could under the circumstances. He also blames his father for the way things are; if only he had encouraged Joe to become an engineer, they would be different and better. He would have been able to provide a stable home for them and gotten them a better education. However, he is not a man who broods over the past; he prefers to plan for his store, and, who knows, he may even get married to have company in his old age.

It was obvious that Joe did not know that Keith, his only son, was serving a ten-year term in a state penitentiary for armed robbery and rape. It was not possible to visit him and he recorded his recollections on a cassette over a period of some months. He recalls his childhood as being sheer hell, spent on a seemingly endless succession of dreary army posts, always too hot or too cold. His father was very hard on him, he feels, always wanting him to do things he did not want to do, or could not do, such as getting all A's in school and being the best lefthanded pitcher on the base. He demanded that Keith learn manual skills, even though he was always clumsy with his hands; still, he was forced to report to the base motor pool and help the mechanics, who only laughed at his awkwardness.

According to Keith, his father was drinking all the time, even though he never acted like a drunk. There were pint bottles of rum concealed all over the house and he was never without his hip flask. He kept in excellent condition, nevertheless, by strenuous exercise, and Keith was forced to follow the same regimen, which bored and exasperated him. He was told at an early age that he was to become an engineer, before he even knew the meaning of the word, and he dreaded that prospect throughout his childhood and early teens. He was unable to get top grades at school—he simply was not smart or industrious enough.

Keith's recollections of his father's wives are dim. The first one did not want any part of the children and spent most of the day drinking beer and watching soap operas; the only words he remembers from her lips were "Go away." The children were still very young then, but they soon learned to look after themselves with Keith being in charge. It was a good thing they did, too, for the second wife on the scene was never home. She spent her days shopping and flirting and paid no more attention to the children than had her predecessor. Keith remembers feeling resentful and bitter, and the brunt of his feelings was aimed at his father, not at his wives. Speaking to the cassette recorder, Keith realized for the first time that his entire childhood was characterized by resentment and bitterness. He resented virtually all the tasks he was expected to perform for his father, he resented the presence of his wives as well as their neglect, and he resented having to look after his sisters.

The only solace Keith had in all that turmoil was music.

He loved listening to the radio and learned to sing along with the singer, and even went to all the band concerts at the base. Music was not taught at school and he had to learn what he could on his own. He played the ukulele first, and then found a guitar somebody had thrown away and taught himself to play it. At every opportunity, he hid in the garage and sang the songs he had heard on the radio to his own accompaniment. All the while, he was dreaming about the time when he would be old enough to leave home and become a country singer.

Keith has received a certain amount of counseling in prison and has gained sufficient insight to realize that he has had sexual problems all his life. At first, it manifested itself in excessive curiosity resulting in habitual voyeurism, which he refined into an art form. He studied the terrain in advance, so that he could prowl in the dark with ease and wear shoes or sneakers best suited for it. In time he pinpointed three or four houses where he could always expect sexual activity and adequate lighting, and every single night he stole out of the house for an hour of voyeurism and masturbation. He wore dark clothes and crawled through bushes on his elbows, the way he had seen soldiers do it in combat training, and he was so adept at concealing himself that he was never caught.

In his teens, he became interested in his sisters. He watched them through the keyhole of the bathroom and managed to drill an almost invisible hole through the ceiling of their bedroom. The schedule set for them by their father was so rigid that Keith knew the exact time they would be undressing each night, and he did not have to waste time waiting. He would time his masturbation so that he came to a climax during the moments they were naked, and then he would sneak out on his nightly prowl to search for conjugal sex scenes. He never became interested in girls and women, and when he raped someone in later years, it was always out of anger, not desire. He blames his father for his sexual problems; he is certain that if he had been provided with a stable home situation and not tormented with unwanted tasks, he would have turned out to be fine.

When he dropped out of high school, he expected his father to be enraged and arranged to be gone by the time he found out about it. He headed for Nashville, fully confident that he was going to find work as a guitar player with a band first, and then as a singer. He was stunned to find out that his guitar playing was woefully amateurish and there was not a chance of his being able to support himself with it. As for his singing, the town was full of country singers waiting for an opportunity, and many of them were a great deal better than he was and yet unemployed. He managed to find enough grubby jobs to keep himself fed and housed, but he was resentful and bitter again at having to do things he did not want to do, and not being able to do what he wanted. This is when he raped a woman for the first time, in the parking lot of a motel, but she was too ashamed to file a complaint and he got away with it. He felt no sexual pleasure—although he claimed this was his first sexual experience with another person—but his anger was dissolved for a few days at least.

Contrary to what his father said, Keith never visited him after he left home. He sent a few postcards with lies of his musical career, but he never gave an address, and after a few years he stopped sending them. He spent those years doing unrewarding work, first in Nashville, later in many other places, and then he began drifting to petty crime as his occupation. He would burglarize isolated houses and occasionally hold up liquor and grocery stores. He always worked alone, wearing a mask, and used extreme caution—as he had in his prowls as a voyeur. He had a gun, but he never hurt anyone, except that every six months or so he raped a woman, always after meticulous planning. After ten years of such life, he raped a liquor store clerk on a whim, following the holdup of the store, and was caught in the act by a passing policeman. He pleaded guilty and was sent to prison for ten years. He is expecting to be paroled soon and feels that his sexual problems have been worked out in counseling and group therapy. He has perfected his guitar playing in prison and plans to look for work as a musician every day, after leaving work in the warehouse job that has been lined up for him. He does not plan to contact his father or sisters.

Nancy is thirty-two and lives near an army base with her second husband—a major—and four children, although her father said she had three. She was exceedingly reluctant to talk about her father and her childhood, and it was apparent that this was the first time she was faced with having to recall painful memories. She loosened up only after several margaritas, but even then she spoke haltingly and only because she thought it might be "therapeutic" for her to talk about matters she had never discussed with anyone.

As a child, Nancy worshiped her father. He was home a lot and kept the children busy even when they were very small; she remembers drying dishes when she could barely hold on to them. Nancy liked that because her stepmothers, who now blend together in her mind, were never around, or so it seemed, and she was often bored and restless. When her father was home, things got exciting and she liked to do whatever he wanted from her. In her recollection, unlike in his, he was not affectionate with Nancy or the other children, and the most she could hope for in the way of reward was a pat on the head and an occasional toy. Toys, however, had to be shared, and when they broke, he would mend them rather than get new ones. Nevertheless, she adored him and believed that he liked her best of all the children.

Nancy also liked living on an army base—the uniforms, the parades, the sense of order, all appealed to her. There were always lots of children to play with, when she had time to play, and later, when she was old enough, lots of boys to date. Later, however, the nature of her relationship with her father changed. Once she started going to school, she was expected to dress immaculately, get good grades, and participate in many extracurricular activities. She was jealous of her sister, who was still young enough to stay home all day, and felt that her father's attention was shifting away from her toward Janet. Like Keith, she was ill-suited to bear the tensions created by her father's demands for participation and excellence, and in time resentment began to prevail over her other feelings toward him.

When she was eleven—the day after her birthday—she was awakened from sleep by her brother, who had slid into her bed. She was not frightened, only surprised, when he guided her hand to his penis and showed her how to masturbate him. In a way, she was pleased that her brother came to her for what she perceived as help, and that she was able to offer it; her only sense of wrongdoing came from the fact that her brother was whispering, so as not to wake up Janet. From then on, his nocturnal visit became an almost nightly event, and for a time she actually looked forward to it and enjoyed it. He always asked her to masturbate him, but he also taught her how to do it to herself, which was an exciting discovery. He extracted a pledge from her never to mention their meetings to anyone, especially Janet and their father, which she was only too glad to give.

Her feelings about their secret activities began to change when she started dating. Nancy thinks now that she might have started dating early because of them, but in any event she lost her virginity at thirteen. After that, his nightly visits turned into an ordeal that she could barely endure. She begged him to stop, but he refused and threatened to expose her to her boyfriends if she did not comply. For two years, she was crushed between unsuccessfully trying to satisfy her father's grinding demands during the day, and her brother's during the night. She found escape only in promiscuous sexuality pursued secretly after school in a "sex club," sheltered in the unsupervised home of a schoolmate.

One afternoon, when Nancy and Keith were alone in the house, she was begging him once again to leave her alone, and he became so infuriated that he raped her, an act he denies. She screamed and tried to resist him, but he seemed so enraged that she was afraid he might hurt her. Afterward, he packed his bags and left the house, never to return. Nancy has not heard from him or seen him since.

She was fifteen at the time, and the next two years of her life are a blur. Although Keith's departure was a tremendous relief to her, she had a compelling urge to tell her secret to someone, and there was no one. She dropped out of school, took a job in town, and moved into a furnished room, whereupon her father forbade her to set foot in his house. Her desperation was total and she abandoned herself to wanton sexuality, mixed with the newfound release of alcohol. At seventeen she became pregnant—she says it was a miracle it had not happened sooner—and the father could have been any one of four or five men she was sleeping with. Acting out of spite and bitterness, she wrote her father a letter and named one of the men as the cause of her pregnancy— the one she liked best. She does not exactly know what Joe might have done, but the man married her soon after.

The marriage did not survive the birth of the baby by a year, and Nancy experienced very hard times after the divorce. Alcoholism and desperate unhappiness led to a nervous breakdown and several years of psychotherapy, and she did not find her way back to a sensible life until she was twenty-seven—after twelve years of unmitigated anguish. She found a good man in her present husband, had three more children, and lives in relative contentment. Her father visited to see his grandchildren a couple of years ago, and their present contact consists of exchanging Christmas cards.

Janet was not available for an extensive talk, and she recorded some of her memories and observations in a letter. She feels that she brought herself up and was untouched by the problems that haunted her brother and sister. She realizes that the competitiveness her father was trying to impose on them was damaging, but she has always felt exempt from it. She was "born much smarter" than her siblings and earned top grades in school without effort, which removed much of the burden of her father's expectations, and she was also a natural athlete, the only one in the family. Janet regards herself as "temperamentally phlegmatic," and if her father's machismo caused any difficulties for her, she is not aware of them.

Janet believes that she had intimidated Keith and Nancy early on and they left her to her own devices. She remembers Keith as having been "secretive and shifty," and Nancy as "vain and hysterical"; they were never affectionate to her and she lacks any warm feelings for them. She views her father dispassionately, too, and described him as a "martinet, a rummy jock," who should never have gotten married. Gratefully, she credits her "genetic endowment" for having been immune to the noxious atmosphere of her home.

Contrary to Joe's assertion that Janet wanders from job to job, she is in fact a highly paid management consultant and "headhunter." She travels 80 percent of the time and drops in on her father when she is in the area and feels like seeing him. She does so principally out of pity, because deep down he must be affected by his disappointment in his children, even though he does not show it. In closing, she notes that her father had no apparent effect on her choice of men; she has very little time for them anyway, and does not intend to get married.

It seems that fathers who can be characterized as macho and/or competitive are more likely to produce unhappy children than fathers with other character traits. Moreover, when children turn out to be not unhappy, the likelihood is that they will be macho and/or competitive themselves. Unlike Kenneth, who developed his macho-competitive qualities as a means of self-defense and adaptation, Joe discerned certain macho traits in his otherwise distant father, adopted them, and expanded them. His competitive aspect was acquired in the army and sharpened by the war through his discovery of the appeal of authority; there is no evidence of it in his father or in his prearmy period.

His mother's invalidism and witnessing his father's casual use of women for sex were influential in honing Joe's evident disdain, if not contempt, for women. He chose his first wife on the grounds of her frailty, a judgment that proved to be fatally correct, the next two out of his need for a housekeeper, and his only goal for his daughters was early marriage.

His aborted wish to become an engineer was foisted on his son with disastrous results, and he compensated for his father's silence and neglect by overwhelming his children. His misperceptions of his children's ability to perform according to his tenets were gross, and today he relies on denial, or adopts his own father's neglect, toward them. He is denying the actual circumstances of his son's departure from home, and has neglected to inform himself on his whereabouts for many years; he does not know how many children his older daughter has; and he does not know that his younger daughter is his only successful child, choosing instead to regard her as an itinerant.

Joe's influence on the formation of his son's perverted sexuality is uncertain, although his failure to provide an adequate mother figure probably had a role in diverting Keith's attention to his sisters and to voyeurism. The same element was instrumental on the destructive experience inflicted on Nancy, and Janet was saved only by her genetic disposition, in her own assessment, which is probably a correct one.

The most noxious factor in the atmosphere created by a macho/competitive father is the resentment he produces in his children, which led to grave consequences for Keith and horrid ones for Nancy. In the absence of such resentment, children like Janet and Donald may escape relatively unharmed, and children like Neil may turn into macho/competitive persons themselves.

bizarre, eccentric

Roy is a most attractive and charming man in his early fifties, impeccably à la mode. He has independent wealth, never worked in his life, and jocularly refers to himself as being educated beyond his intelligence, without giving credit to Oscar Wilde. He regards the moral standards observed by society as obsolete and quickly makes it known that he is an amoral hedonist who believes that everything, absolutely everything, is permissible so long as it is private. He is proud of the fact that his father committed suicide two months before Roy was born, because, as he wrote in his final note, he could not face impending fatherhood. He is no less proud of his mother, who chose not to grieve and married his father's best friend when Roy was six weeks old, placing the infant in the trusteeship of a guardian. Roy believes that his parents were a pair of dashing romantics, sort of Zelda–Scott types without the insanity and the booze, and views his own fate as an infant as a "Dickensian tableau."

His guardian was a most benevolent pillar of society who provided Roy with the best environment money and taste could buy, and gave permission to Roy's all but most nefarious requests so long as he was left in peace himself. Roy was coddled by the best of nannies and assorted domestics under the supervision of a housekeeper, and spent his first six years in a household of servants where he was the pampered guest. Better yet, his parents had "the foresight" of having virtually no relatives, and his paradisical existence was immune to incursions by interested uncles and aunts who could only have confused the peaceful household with inquiries and conflicting instructions.

As a result of continuous coddling, Roy was equipped with a fortified ego upon entering a fashionable boarding school at the age of six and was able to withstand the rigors of fagging and other traditional indignities without lasting damage. In due course, he became an upperclassman and developed into a "virtuoso sadist," inventing physically harmless but humiliating penances for the boys in the lower grades. One of his favorites was forcing boys to lick his shoes clean before allowing them to proceed to the dining room, or seizing some valued property and returning it only after the victim had crawled through deep snow on his hands and knees.

Meanwhile, he was receiving an excellent education without much effort, for his mind was like a sponge and he was altogether enjoying himself. The school was his world; he was totally familiar with its every angle and crevice and he felt totally free within its walls. During Christmas recess, when other boys who were saddled by parents and families had to endure the seasonal rituals in their homes, Roy was allowed to stay on with the housekeeping staff. He really liked sleeping in a different room every night, roaming the empty corridors, having the library to himself, eating with the grown-ups—he felt like a prince in his castle. When the others came back, he extracted his dues from their holiday goodies and made them tell tales of what they had endured.

Summers were the bane of his existence. His guardian arranged for him to go abroad each summer, a different country every year, and stay with a native family he had selected. The objective was for Roy to immerse himself in the culture of the country and perfect his knowledge of languages, but he abhorred living with strangers in strange houses. The only redeeming quality of summers was that they provided sexual opportunities that were unavailable in boarding school. There was a homosexuality clique at school, its membership changing each year, and Roy has had minor sexual encounters with boys, but they were unsatisfactory to him and he did not yearn to explore further. What he yearned for were the sultry women he had first seen in Spain when he was only nine and in Italy when he was eleven, but he had to wait till he was fifteen before this yearning was to be fulfilled.

The outbreak of World War II put an end to European summers and it was arranged for Roy to spend his vacations on the ranch of a wealthy landowner in a South American country each year. Much as he disliked familial settings, he became strongly attracted to the oldest daughter of the family he was staying with as soon as he set eyes on her—he was fourteen, she eighteen. The summer was spent in leashed passion, for the girl had many admirers who had more to offer than a young boy could, and Roy's suffering was intense. It carried over into the following school year, most of which he spent in dreaming about Yvette, and for the first time in his life he was counting the days till the coming summer. He spent a great deal of time working on his physique, even though he was overdeveloped for his age, because he discovered that during the teen years being bigger was equivalent to being older. He spent hours each day hanging from doorways by his fingers with weights tied to his feet, in the hope of adding a couple of inches to his stature. The course of nature added to his own efforts produced a robust appearance by the time summer came, and Roy was convinced that he looked at least seventeen. Indeed, Yvette greeted him with an observation about his sudden maturity and spoke to him more often during the first two days than she had all the previous summer. Roy was ecstatic and made up his mind to seduce Yvette.

He had informed himself a long time ago on what a man was expected to do with a woman, and in his fantasies during the previous year he had prepared every move in advance—he choreographed his first night with Yvette. He decided to gamble on success rather than wait for an opportunity that may never come, and on the fifth night he stole into Yvette's room. He thought he would pass himself off as a dream, and indeed she responded to his initial caresses without awaking, emboldening him to proceed with his long-rehearsed plan. His success was complete and he felt delirious with joy as he stole out of Yvette's room, leaving her sleeping as peacefully as she was when he came in.

Yvette gave no sign of being aware of what had happened during the next day, and if she was, she concealed it perfectly. Roy avoided looking at her or talking to her all day and he was feverishly preparing his plan of action for the next night. He was getting ready to pay his second visit as the long-awaited hour arrived when his door opened and Yvette came in, fully dressed. She turned off the lights and whispered, "Yvette was a bad girl last night. You must punish her," and slipped a lasso used by the gauchos in his hands. She instructed him to deliver ten lashes across her backside, leaving on her clothes to prevent lash marks and blood. He was stunned at first and then reluctant, compelling Yvette to beg him on her knees, but he agreed at last and found that after the first two or three lashings the act became more and more enjoyable. Yvette responded passionately and when he completed the task, he begged her to do the same to him.

For the rest of the summer, an unvarying ritual was played out by Roy and Yvette. He would go to her room every other night and make love to her as much as he wanted, while she would feign sleep through it all. On alternate nights, she would come to his room, beg for punishment, receive it, and reciprocate, after which she would return to her room. Roy found the arrangement perfectly suited to his temperament, and in time came to prefer the lashings. They perfected their technique and expanded it both in duration and intensity, and by the end of the summer Roy was a confirmed sadomasochist.

Yvette got married during the following winter and Roy

never saw her again, but the experience established a pattern for his sexual future. He relates proudly that when he went back to school with his new skills, he initiated a couple of boys, and the three of them spent many happy hours together during the school year. He obtained various refined instruments through the mail, and they devised new "exercises" to enhance pleasure; their only rule was not to inflict exercises if the other was unwilling. After he finished boarding school and entered college, he always kept an eye out for willing partners, and he was seldom without one. With women, he liked to alternate sex with sadomasochism whenever they were willing; with men he avoided sex altogether and engaged in a much wider range of exercises. He formed a small group and set meetings at regular hours and days, endowing it with a sense of permanence. He felt closer to members of the group than to anyone—he says they were his first family.

After graduating from college, he embarked on a career of travel, and as time went on he established similar groups in various cities that he liked to frequent, so that whenever he returned he had a surrogate family waiting for him and he did not have to feel like a stranger. He also found women in these cities, and set some of them up in apartments of his choosing, for which he paid the rent. Thus he traveled around the world, moving from family to family, nest to nest, doing nothing but seeking and finding pleasure. He assumed control of his inherited wealth at twenty-one, and had no one to account to, no one to explain his actions to, no one to look over his shoulder. When he was not on the move, he read prodigiously, always discarding books as soon as he finished them, and in time he refined his life to the point where he did not even have to carry luggage. He had one of everything he needed in every place he visited.

When he was in his late twenties, one of his women "on location"—a Spanish one, like the object of his earliest desire—became pregnant by him, an assertion confirmed by his scrutiny of the calendar and his travel schedule, and insisted on giving birth to the baby. At first, he had a moment of panic and contemplated abandoning the woman, fearing that he might be tempted to follow his father's example, but it passed, and he decided that it might be "diverting" to have a child to visit. He made it a point to be present when the baby was born, and made elaborate and lavish arrangements for the mother's homecoming from the hospital, followed by a sumptuous party at the best hotel; since the baby was a boy, he gave the mother a generous "bonus."

The baby was to be a five-year-old boy named Albert when his father visited him next. To his astonishment, Roy found the experience "terribly moving and interesting," and he took to the boy immediately. Albert looked very much like his father and he was very sharp and smart, so Roy decided to "make a major investment in him." He entered him in one of Europe's best boarding schools, retained a local attorney to look after Albert's interests while he was in school, and bought an elegant seaside villa for the boy's mother, so that mother and son could spend school holidays together. Meanwhile, as his investment was maturing, Roy continued to lead his customary life, traveling leisurely, ever refining his sadomasochistic pleasures, keeping his sexuality keen by acquiring new women and replacing old ones, but now he had in Albert a long-range interest he had never had before.

He still had no feeling for anything familial and had no plans for settling in one place with one woman, or even one of his groups. Nor did he even think of Albert as his son, but as a potential heir and successor to whom he would one day hand over his princely realm, if he was deserving, and he was determined to make sure that he would be. He visited the boy's school once a year, held elaborate consultations with the headmaster on matters of curriculum, and spent a day with Albert, checking on his progress by questioning him in several languages about what he had been learning. In the summertime, he usually managed to get to the seaside villa for three or four days to see how Albert conducted himself when he was away from school, and kept a sharp eye out for any indications of the direction of the boy's sexuality. He also questioned the mother on the subject and instructed her to be on the lookout for signs and symptoms.

He freely admits to having planned to form the boy in his own image, because that is the most desirable image he knew. He does not conceal his extreme fondness of himself, and he is certain that he has never done anything that should make him feel regretful or ashamed. If not all his endeavors have succeeded, the fault was never his, as far as he could discern. He does not consider himself perfect by any means, but is convinced that his "gestalt is perfectly consistent and without self-contradictions." He claims never to have been depressed or in anguish over anything, or even to feel anxiety; he has had an ideal life over which he had complete control, and he felt uniquely equipped to re-create himself in Albert.

When Albert reached the age of thirteen, Roy decided that the time was right for taking him along on his journeys during the summer vacation. The boy was quite mature for his age, but had had no sexual experiences beyond the daily masturbations reported by his mother; Roy felt that he was ready to experience pleasure, or at least ready to find out if he had capacity for it. He planned the itinerary with care, selecting only stops where the boy would be received and treated with sensitivity and tact, and allowed to feel his way around on his own, though not without Roy's supervision and guidance. The first city chosen was Paris, because he had extensive contacts there, ranging from his own "woman on location" and local "family" to *demimondaines* and purveyors of all imaginable services. Also, he was not unmindful of the excitement Paris could generate for a thirteen-year-old boy, nor of its cultural and aesthetic allure.

He guided Albert in the conventional manner during their first few days there, meanwhile probing for clues to his level of sexual sophistication. To his surprise, the boy was not at all shy or reticent on the subject, volunteering the information that he was theoretically knowledgeable on the subject, having consulted not only treatises on sex but also medical books and anatomical atlases. Alas, he was completely lacking in practical experience, but felt quite ready to immerse himself in it. When Roy suggested that Albert permit him to arrange the details of his sexual initiation, he agreed gratefully and Roy immediately put into effect the plan he had devised. A young woman of considerable experience, once kept by Roy, was chosen as most suited to the occasion, both on account of his relative youth and her enthusiasm when the details of the plan were broached to her. An intimate dinner *à trois* was arranged for the following night, and Albert was told to prepare himself.

Unlike other fathers who have seen to the introduction of a son to sexual experience by employing a prostitute or a willing volunteer and then letting her do what was required, Roy took the matter in his own hands completely. He could not trust any woman in such a crucial act; after all, it was not only his heir presumptive but his own to be re-created self that was involved, and any mistake could be costly later in Albert's life. Consequently, when the splendid food and wines had mellowed their senses, he proceeded to demonstrate to Albert the ways of lovemaking, beginning with the kiss. He and Celeste had the boy observe them closely as they played out the repertory of kissing, and when he was ready to take over, and he showed no reticence in the matter, he moved over to his father's place on the sofa. After he proved to be an apt student, Roy demonstrated the next phase, then the next, until the boy was thoroughly initiated. "For an encore," says Roy, father and son joined to make love to Celeste together.

Roy was tremendously relieved that Albert was so complaisant and he was ready to introduce him to other aspects of his life. He instructed members of his local group to act in a restrained fashion upon meeting Albert, to hold back, so as not to frighten him, and everything went swimmingly. Not only did the boy catch on very quickly but soon he was initiating contacts and acting like a pro. Roy says it was the first time in his life that he felt proud of someone other than himself, and from then on nothing was withheld from the boy. His father took him everywhere, showed him everything, and the reaction to Albert was exceedingly favorable, even enthusiastic. Women loved the ardent young man, men lusted after him, but explicit homosexual activity was forbidden by Roy. He himself had never desired it, and he did not want to overload Albert with too great a variety of sexual experiences too soon. If he were to choose homosexuality later in life, that would be acceptable, but not yet. The travels of the first summer concluded, he took Albert back to school, but not without repeatedly emphasizing the value of being well educated. If he wanted to become a man of the world, a good education was absolutely essential, for the full enjoyment of pleasure requires a frame of reference only education can provide. It was not that Albert resisted going back to school, but Roy wanted him to know and remember what great stress he was placing on it.

The pattern was set for the following eight years; Albert in school, later college, during the school year, and with his father for the summer. He saw his mother only for Christmas and Easter vacations and when she visited him at school. The arrangement seemed to be very satisfactory to all, and all thrived; Albert was becoming his father's equal in hedonism, and the influence his mother has had over him in matters of religion was waning. The time was not far off when he would equal Roy in amorality as well. Roy was somewhat uncomfortable at being apparently idolized, a feeling he has never experienced himself and did not know what to do with. He did not think that his feelings toward Albert were similar to what he imagined other fathers felt toward their sons, but he was unable to verbalize them when he was prompted. He did feel pride, but it was more the pride of a teacher for a star pupil; he did feel admiration, but more for Albert's accomplishments than for his person. Aside from enjoying and playing variations on the theme of pleasure together, he knew little about other aspects of his son's life, nor had he much interest in them. If Albert wondered much about his father's pursuits during the rest of the year, he did not express it.

Their relationship began to change subtly after Albert turned twenty-one and took control of the substantial trust fund Roy had set up for him years before. He finished his undergraduate studies at an English university, but surprised Roy by announcing that he wanted to work for a doctorate in archeology, in which he had been long interested. There

177

was no reason to oppose his plans, and Roy did not, although it was obviously going to cut into their time together. The first year of graduate school in America deprived Roy of a full month of his son's company in the summer, as he spent that time on a dig in the Middle East. In the second year, Albert's enthusiasm for pleasure-seeking seemed to pall, and when his father questioned him, he admitted to being somewhat satiated. Roy was taken aback, but decided to hold back until Albert finished his studies in the hope that this condition was temporary; it was unimaginable to him that one, especially his own son, could lose interest in sensual pleasure.

In the third year, Albert had a confession to make; it seems that ever since the night of his initiation when he was thirteen, he could not get Celeste out of his mind, and after all those years he finally decided to seek her out. He found her easily in Paris, where she was then the mistress of an industrialist, and she admitted to him that she, too, had often thought about him. One thing led to another, and right now Celeste is living with Albert in his beach house near the university. True, she is eight years older than he, but she is still only thirty-two and Albert is in love with her; he has had enough variety for a lifetime, he said, and just wanted to stay with Celeste.

Roy was first astonished, then furious, but did not show it. He knew that all his plans went awry, that all those years of effort to re-create himself were for nothing, and that something had to be done. He was devastated, which was again a new experience for him, and the more he thought about Albert, the angrier he became. He plotted elaborate plans of revenge, some admittedly mad, but he was too stunned to act. He indulged in hedonistic activities to the point of being out of control, and for a "cure," he retraced the first journey he had taken with Albert, taking pains to seek out the same people they were involved with, the same women they had shared. It helped somewhat, and he was on his way back to America when he got word that Albert had been killed in a motorcycle accident on the West Coast.

He had never felt grief before, and he is not sure that he

did then. There was for a moment a flash of triumph, he winks, the triumph of surviving one's son, but it gave way to profound sadness, similar to the feelings he had had years ago on the death of a friend. There was also a feeling of loss, and when he saw Albert's coffin being lowered to the grave, he knew that nothing would be the same again.

Immediately after the funeral, he persuaded Celeste to come and live with him and during the first couple of months together he experienced a pitch of sexual excitement and fulfillment with her that surpassed every sexual and sensual act he had ever had. It did not last beyond that, but they have been together two years now. He has reduced his traveling to be with her more, and sometimes they travel together just like tourists. He has resigned himself to Albert's death and regained his composure; "It is all in McFate's hands," he said, again failing to credit the author of his quip.

Two months after Roy related the story of his son, he died of an overdose of heroin—one form of pleasure he did not admit to pursuing. He was in every sense the author of his own life, and the death he wrote for himself was a master stroke; it brought to full cycle what began with his father's suicide for fear of an heir, and ended with his own for the loss of one. It is a classic story, stark in outline and gothic in ornamentation.

Roy was without ancestors and spent his life avoiding the sprouting of roots. He created an aura for his parents and turned himself loose to fabricate his own persona out of thin air. His rules were minimal: Do not form ties; dissolve the pain of abandonment in pools of pleasure. Money made it easier for him than it might have been without it, and so did a quick mind and a sound education. He could intellectualize feelings before they had time to form and hurt him, he could hop on a plane to escape them, he could drown them in champagne or sensuality. His was not a first-rate mind and he had to borrow most of his props elsewhere in designing his life. All was built on the need to conceal his primal pain and his irreparable loneliness—the ready wit, the immersion in books, and the insatiable body. But, then, we must not forget that no one could have been lonelier than Roy: without parents, without family, growing like a plant in the deserted boarding school.

The pampering of the early years endowed him with total self-confidence, albeit an artificial one, and it filled up his interior like a balloon. It lifted him above doubts and anxieties, it enabled him to feel perfect, and nothing could have been more tempting than the wish to re-create himself, except this time with roots. Psychoanalysts might note that in being father to his son and merging with him by means of shared women he also became his own father. When the stratagem failed and Albert veered away from the path laid out for him, Roy was already doomed; his death merely hastened the end.

Three other families were encountered that could be designated as "bizarre, eccentric" but their stories could not be used. So pronounced were their eccentricities that it was impossible to disguise them without violating their authenticity, and without disguise they would have been easily identifiable. They had one thing in common. Every family had one son or daughter who remained immune to unseemly or outrageous behavior by the father. Like Albert or Donald, they ultimately forged their own character and went their own way—sometimes forgiving, sometimes rejecting, just like all other children.

ABOUT THE AUTHOR

Robert Meister is a prolific writer whose work covers a wide range of subjects. He is a former columnist for the *Journal of Existentialism*, and was the ghost writer on all of the late Theodore Reik's books written between the early fifties and his death, including the bestselling LISTENING WITH THE THIRD EAR. He has also written numerous articles for *Pyschology Today*, *Self*, and *Mademoiselle*.